Prader-Willi Homes of Oconomowoc (PWHO) specializes in providing residential services and supports to individuals diagnosed with Prader-Willi Syndrome (PWS). For over 35 years, PWHO has been nationally and internationally recognized by the PWS community for excellence in the therapeutic treatment and care for individuals diagnosed with PWS, and now supports more individuals diagnosed with PWS than any other residential provider in the world.

Prader-Willi Homes of Oconomowoc /
Admissions Director
P.O. Box 278
Dousman, WI 53118
262-569-4848
http://www.pwho.com

INSATIABLE

INSATIABLE

A PRADER-WILLI STORY

THE ORP LIBRARY

WRITTEN BY
DEBBIE FRISK
CHELSEA McCUTCHIN
WITH
JAMES G. BALESTRIERI
KATIE GUTIERREZ

WRITERS OF THE ROUND TABLE PRESS
PO BOX 511
HIGHLAND PARK, IL 60035

Publisher	COREY MICHAEL BLAKE
Executive Editor	KATIE GUTIERREZ
Creative Director	DAVID CHARLES COHEN
Director of Operations	KRISTIN WESTBERG
Facts Keeper	MIKE WINICOUR
Cover Design	ANALEE PAZ
Interior Design	SUNNY DIMARTINO
Interior Layout	KRISTY LINGEBACH, SUNNY DIMARTINO
Proofreading	RITA HESS
Last Looks	SUNNY DIMARTINO
Digital Book Conversion	SUNNY DIMARTINO
Digital Publishing	SUNNY DIMARTINO

Printed in the United States of America
First Edition: September 2014
10 9 8 7 6 5 4 3 2 1

Library of Congress Cataloging-in-Publication Data
Frisk, Debbie
Insatiable: a prader-willi story /
Debbie Frisk, Chelsea McCutchin.—1st ed. p. cm.
Print ISBN: 978-1-939418-67-8   Digital ISBN: 978-1-939418-68-5
Library of Congress Control Number: 2014949274
Number 10 in the series: The ORP Library
The ORP Library: Insatiable

RTC Publishing is an imprint of Writers of the Round Table, Inc.
Writers of the Round Table Press and the RTC Publishing logo
are trademarks of Writers of the Round Table, Inc.

CONTENTS

The real visionary behind Prader-Willi Homes of Oconomowoc is a woman named Dorothy Foulkes. A gifted special educator, administrator, and RN, Dorothy was working with children with PWS in the 60s and 70s when very little was known about the syndrome. This book is dedicated to her, in the fervent hope that those she taught have made her proud.

INTRODUCTION

Today, according to the U.S. Department of Health and Human Services, more than 5.5 million children—or eight percent of kids—in the U.S. have some form of disability. Whether the problem is physical, behavioral, or emotional, these children struggle to communicate, learn, and relate to others. While there is no longer *segregation* in the same sense as there was in the 1950s, what remains the same is the struggle. Even with all of our resources and technology, parents of children with disabilities fight battles every day to find the help and education their children need.

I have led Oconomowoc Residential Programs (ORP) for almost thirty years. We're a family of companies offering specialized services and care for children, adolescents, and adults with disabilities. Too often, when parents of children with disabilities try to find funding for programs like ours, they are bombarded by red tape, conflicting information, or no information at all, so they struggle blindly for years to secure an appropriate education. Meanwhile, home life, and the child's wellbeing, suffers. In cases when parents and caretakers have exhausted their options—and their hope—ORP is here to help. We felt it was time to offer parents a new, unexpected tool to fight back: stories that educate, empower, and inspire.

The original idea was to create a library of comic books that could empower families with information to reclaim their rights. We wanted to give parents and caretakers the information they need to advocate for themselves, as well as provide educators and therapists with a therapeutic tool. And, of course, we wanted to reach the children—to offer them a visual representation of their journey that would show that they aren't alone, nor are they wrong or "bad" for their differences. What we found in the process of writing original stories for the comics is that these journeys are too long, too complex, to be contained within a standard comic. So what we are now creating is an ORP library of disabilities books—traditional books geared toward parents, caretakers, educators, and therapists, *and* comic books portraying the world through the eyes of children with disabilities. Both styles of books share what we have learned while advocating for families over the years while also honestly highlighting their emotional journeys. We're creating communication devices that anyone can read to understand complex disabilities in a new way.

In an ideal situation, these books will be used therapeutically, to communicate the message, and to help support the work ORP and companies like ours are doing. The industry has changed dramatically and is not likely to turn around any time soon—certainly not without more people being aware of families' struggles. We have an opportunity to put a face to the conversation, reach out to families, and start that dialogue.

Caring for children with disabilities consumes your life. We know that. And we want you to realize, through these stories, that you are not alone. We can help.

Sincerely,
Jim Balestrieri
CEO, Oconomowoc Residential Programs
www.orplibrary.com

A NOTE ABOUT THIS BOOK

Prader-Willi Syndrome is a complex disorder that affects children, teens, and adults in different ways. The child with Prader-Willi Syndrome in this book struggles with physical, emotional, and behavioral challenges that require a therapeutic environment. At Prader-Willi Homes of Oconomowoc, we strive to build relationships with our clients and collaborate with their families to teach them skills that will contribute to healthier, safer, and happier lives. It is our hope that this book will add to your own understanding of the often-lonely journey of families experiencing these unique challenges—and gifts.

PROLOGUE

"Ian! Ian!" Samantha's voice broke through the thick sleep that Ian had drifted into immediately after his eyes fluttered shut. He jumped out of the recliner that he'd placed outside his daughter's room, where he'd been sitting every night for the past week. He and Samantha had been taking turns keeping guard, and he was a physical and emotional wreck.

"What? Did I fall asleep? It couldn't have been for more than a minute . . ." Ian dropped his sentence as he looked at the clock. Shit! he thought. The last time he'd looked, it had read a quarter to one. Now it was almost five a.m.

"Never mind that. Where is she?" Samantha asked, her eyes wide. "Where is Violet?" She gestured aggressively to the open door of Violet's room, pointing to the rumpled sheets and silence that indicated their daughter's absence.

"I don't—" Ian's blood ran cold at the thought that she'd escaped, again.

"You only had one job, Ian!" Samantha rushed her husband, beating on his chest with her fists. She was equally exhausted, and while she knew, logically, that Ian wasn't to blame for Violet sneaking out, she had to place the blame somewhere. Ian caught his wife's fists in his hands.

"Stop it, Sam. Stop!" His voice was firm, and although he was fighting back tears; he knew he had to be the one to hold it together. "If she's not in the house, we have to call the police. We can't do this anymore."

Samantha fell to the floor with Ian's comment. She sobbed like a child, her insecurities liquefied and falling in heavy drops.

"Violet? Baby are you here?" Ian called out, stepping over his crumpled wife. He could only deal with one crisis at a time now, and his patience with Samantha's dramatics had worn thin over the past eighteen years. "Violet?" Ian rushed to the garage door to find that the home alarm was still activated from the inside. She hadn't left the house, and he breathed a silent sigh of relief. Listening, he heard footsteps upstairs; his daughter's lumbering weight betrayed her on the heavy wooden floors in their century-old row home. Ian crept over to the stairs. "Vi?" With each step up, his trepidation built. Where would he find his daughter? What would she be doing?

"I'm not here, Dad!" Her voice came from the hall bathroom.

Ian flung open the door. Violet was sitting on the countertop, leaning over the sink. An empty bottle of Pepto Bismol rested on the counter, and Violet's pink mustache betrayed that she'd guzzled the bottle like a milkshake. She'd picked a bald spot on her head, and her scalp and fingernails were caked in dried blood.

"Violet, you—" Ian didn't even know where to begin. He looked down at her arms and, to his horror, realized that the blood embedded in Violet's fingernails wasn't just from her scalp but dripping from the deep cuts she'd inflicted upon her left arm.

"Baby, what did you do?" Ian rushed over to his daughter.

"My arm bothers me." Violet looked at her father quizzically, leaned into him, and passed out.

"Samantha!" Ian cried into the hallway. "Samantha! Get up and call an ambulance!"

Ian pulled Violet into his arms as he surveyed the scene around him. He saw the pink razor in the sink: Violet had taken the plastic safety sleeve off and used the blades to shred her skin. The scene was overwhelming, and while trying to piece everything together, it hit him. A few days ago, Violet had been bitten by a mosquito. She just couldn't leave the welt alone, and for days Ian and his wife had been placing socks over her hands to keep her from picking and scratching at night. Her obsessive-compulsive tendencies had finally taken over, and Violet had decided to dig at the bite with a razor. He shook his head, letting out a breath that was half-growl and half-sob. As a psychiatrist, Ian knew that the emergency room doctors would treat Violet like a case of attempted suicide. While he could try to explain that his daughter was more than an angst-ridden teenager, it was damn near impossible to explain Violet's condition to each doctor she met. Ian had to divorce himself from his role of father and go into crisis mode.

"Where is she?" Samantha appeared at the door and shrieked at the sight of her bloody daughter laid out across her husband's chest.

"Sam, call an ambulance. She's going to be okay." Ian kept his voice calm. "Just call 911."

Samantha stood dumbstruck for a moment before rushing down the hall to get the phone. Meanwhile, Ian pulled Violet from the countertop and cradled her on the floor. He yanked a towel from the bar above him and applied pressure to her arm. The skin was flaked back, and while she'd cut through all the layers, she hadn't reached a major vein or artery. While Dr. Durkin prepared to talk to the police and the EMTs who would arrive shortly, a father's tears wet his daughter's face.

CHAPTER 1

Samantha rolled over to her left side and rubbed her tight, swollen belly. In less than a month, she could use the tiny pink onesies and socks with lace that she'd so carefully picked out months ago. She was finally having the little girl she'd always wanted. And God, she couldn't wait. This was her third pregnancy, and her daughter was giving her more trouble than her boys ever had: weekly urine tests, monthly ultrasounds, a recommended amniocentesis at twenty weeks, and the God-awful gestational diabetes test with the thick drink that went down like Tang-flavored syrup—not just once, but twice.

She stared at the television, where three people were yelling, arguing about who fathered the little boy shown on a screen above them, before grabbing the remote control and turning it off. *I went to Harvard for this?* she thought, half-smiling to keep her tears at bay. Everything had been going so well. Lukas was four years old and Mitchell eighteen months, and Samantha and Ian had embraced the often-exhausting role of parents. Then last week, she'd made excuses to cut a meeting short at her PR firm, mortified because she thought she'd wet her pants. She went to the ladies' room and found her panties almost blood-soaked. That was all she remembered before she passed out.

She awoke to Ian standing by her hospital bed, tears in his eyes. Terrified that something was wrong with her baby, she shot straight into a sitting position.

"What's going on? Why am I here?"

"You and our baby are going to be okay," Ian reassured her, tucking her chin-length blonde hair behind her ear. "Dr. Thompson is coming in to talk to us in just a few minutes."

As if on cue, Samantha's OB-GYN entered the hospital room, holding her chart.

"Samantha, you gave us all quite a scare," he said.

"What's going on?" she asked, with no regard for his pleasantries.

"Looks like your placenta has shifted closer to your cervix than we'd like. Your bag of waters is still intact, but we need you to stay here until you deliver."

Samantha looked from Dr. Thomson to Ian, laughing shortly. "That's unacceptable. I can't stay here. I have two toddlers at home, and I have to finalize everything at work next week before I take my maternity leave."

"Samantha." Ian smiled at his wife, but his voice was firm. "My two favorite girls are in this bed, and they're going to stay here until I can bring them both home safely."

Samantha rolled her eyes. At thirty-seven, she knew that she was at an increased risk for complications. This was her first pregnancy where her midwife insisted that she go to a traditional obstetrician, due to her age. Lukas had been born in a hospital, with natural, unassisted labor, Mitchell was born in a birthing center, and Samantha was determined that her little girl would complete her ultimate goal: being born at home in the water.

"I need to talk to Abby, my midwife. I need her here to advocate for me," Samantha said, not backing down. "You can't hold me in this hospital. I was designed to give birth. My body was made for this, and I refuse to . . ."

"Yes, you were," Ian said. "But right now you need a little help. There's a reason that hospitals and obstetrics were invented. For special cases. You and our little girl are a special case right now. Just relax. I'll bring the boys up here to visit with you every day."

Samantha rolled her eyes again, indignant. She was a lot of things, but a "special case" was not one of them. "I'll do what I have to do for now, but as soon as this bleeding stops, I'm going home."

"Samantha, we've stopped the bleeding with a cerclage of your cervix," Dr. Thomson said. "But you're going to have to stay here until it's time to deliver. We want to give the baby as much time in the oven as we can." Dr. Thompson's eyes were kind, though his tone indicated that he was growing annoyed by Samantha's arguments.

"You stitched up my cervix?" Samantha was furious. "Without my consent?"

Dr. Thompson looked over to Ian. He wasn't going to argue with Samantha anymore.

"I consented, Samantha," Ian said. "You and the baby were losing a lot of blood. It saved you both." Ian leaned down to his wife, stroking her hair with the tips of his fingers.

"I need to rest now. That's what I'm supposed to be doing, right?" Samantha brushed Ian's hand away and rolled over, facing away from him. She didn't want her husband or the doctor to see the tears that were now spilling down her cheeks. Her natural home birth was being taken from her. In an instant, her fantasy of how she would bring her daughter, the next generation of woman, into the world dissolved, leaving her feeling angry and helpless.

Over ten days, Samantha got used to hospital bed rest, at least as used to it as she could. Lying in a bed all day alone was abject misery. She missed her boys and her job, but she was trying to be a good patient and let her baby get ready to be born. She rubbed her belly again. "You'll come when you're ready, but the sooner the better, okay, little girl? We're full term now and I want to take you home." She felt a slight shift in her belly, more like butterflies fluttering than a full-term baby moving. She imagined that her little girl was rolling over, a gentle, lazy movement.

Her daughter never kicked her as her boys did. With Lukas, she felt elbows and knees running against her ribs and hipbones every night. Mitchell seemed to hook his toes into her ribs and bang his head against her bladder as hard as he could. She smiled at the memory; her sons already had their personalities in utero. Lukas was naturally curious and exploratory. Mitchell was impatient and brash, trying like hell to escape any limits or expectations placed on him. But this little girl seemed content to hang out, occasionally rolling around to let Samantha know she was okay. When she'd brought it up to Dr. Thompson, he just told her that she was now housing the fairer sex and that every pregnancy was different. Samantha was relieved that she wasn't losing sleep while her child kicked field goals, but a little more movement would have been reassuring.

Now bored, Samantha paged the nurse. She didn't have to go to the bathroom, but at least walking to the toilet would give her something to do. Roxanne, a middle-aged woman with hair that Samantha described to Ian as "fire engine red" appeared at the door.

"Time to use the facilities again, Samantha?" Roxanne gave Samantha a knowing wink.

"Yep. Time again." Samantha smiled, starting to pull herself from the bed. She sat on the side and slid her feet into the plush slippers that Ian had bought her to make her more comfortable at the hospital. They were two sizes bigger than her normal shoes, but her feet were so swollen that it was getting difficult to squeeze them into the soft cotton. As soon as she stood, she felt a shift inside, and liquid trickled down her leg, dampening the light pink slippers.

"Oops, guess I had to go more than I thought." Samantha managed an uncomfortable smile at the nurse, mortified that she'd urinated before she reached the toilet. In the next second, though, she remembered that sudden, warm gush of water breaking that took everyone by surprise. "Or is it—"

"Let's take a look at that," Roxanne said, moving closer.

Samantha shifted, but when she tried to walk, she doubled over with pain. In moments, she was on all fours on the cold tile floor.

Roxanne dropped to her knees beside Samantha. "Yup, that was your water, Sam. Let's get you back on the bed and call Dr. Thompson."

"Can I walk? My labors move faster if I'm able to walk around," Samantha said, breathing through the pain. "Call Ian."

"No, ma'am. I'll call Ian, but you need to get back into the bed until the doctor gets here." Roxanne put Samantha's arm around her neck and picked her up, leading her to the bed. Once Samantha was lying down, Roxanne rushed out of the room.

Samantha's contraction had subsided, and she took the moment to press on her belly with her fingers. She wanted her daughter to give her some sort of sign that she was ready to go. In Samantha's previous pregnancies, she felt as though she'd been able to read her sons; her mind and body just *knew* when the boys were ready to meet the world. With this child, Samantha felt disconnected, as if even the baby didn't know what she wanted to do. So, when her daughter didn't respond to the pressure of Samantha's fingertips, she was disappointed but not surprised.

Ten minutes later, a woman Samantha didn't recognize ran into the room, accompanied by the nurses Samantha had grown to know over the past week and a half.

"Who are you?" Samantha demanded of the woman, writhing in pain. Her contractions were coming on top of each other now.

"Dr. Soto. I'm the obstetrician on call right now from Dr. Thompson's practice." The woman lifted Samantha's hospital gown and performed a cervical check. "It's time," Dr. Soto said, her face stoic.

"I don't even know you! What do you think you're doing?" Samantha tried to pull away from the doctor's hand but was overtaken with another contraction and almost forgot about the woman completely.

"Have you called Ian?" Samantha managed when the

contraction passed, looking at Roxanne.

"He's on his way." Roxanne rubbed Samantha's knee. "Right now, we're going to move you to a labor suite. Get ready for the ride."

Samantha laid back and watched the fluorescent lights of the hospital fly over her head as her bed was rolled down the hallway. Suddenly, a spotlight shone on her body, and her feet were positioned into stirrups.

"I need you to push, Sam." Roxanne was by her side. "One, two, three . . ." Samantha lost all concept of time as her primal nature took over, and by God, she was going to deliver this baby. Soon, Ian was by her side, his hand on her shoulder.

"You got this Sam. You can do it." His voice was familiar and firm in his belief in her.

Samantha found her focus and pulled up her torso to give the push everything she had. From a great distance away, she heard a woman wailing, her voice sounding as if it were being ripped from her chest. Vaguely, Samantha felt sorry for the woman, before she realized the sound was coming from her own mouth.

"Is she okay?" she heard Ian ask. "She's never been like this before."

"She's bleeding, doctor. Is that a hemorrhage?" A nurse's voice joined the din, but Samantha pushed it out of her mind, focusing on her delivery and her strength, just as she'd been taught by the midwife before Lukas's birth— and damn it, where *was* her midwife?

"I'm getting worried. This is her third child, right?" Samantha heard Dr. Soto's voice. "We've been pushing for almost two hours. She's already lost a lot of blood. I think it's time to call for a section."

Ian rubbed Samantha's leg. "Do it. Do whatever you have to do."

"No!" Samantha's mind was racing. She was utterly exhausted. All she heard was "bleeding" and "section," followed by Ian agreeing with a doctor who, in her mind, wanted to butcher her. She thought of the tears of joy she should be crying with her baby in her arms. She thought of her two babies at home. At that moment, her adrenaline rushed and her tolerance for anything else was gone. Frantically, she called out, "Ian! Ian! Help me!" Just then, an anesthesiologist appeared and placed a mask over Samantha's face. She tried to fight him off but was so tired that her arms couldn't reflect the same determination and strength that shone in her eyes.

"Breathe, Samantha," the doctor said. "Just breathe."

...

Samantha woke up and looked around the room. She was groggy but couldn't remember ever sleeping so well at the hospital. She scanned the room and saw Ian sitting on the daybed the hospital provided for fathers and guests. He was leaning forward, eyes closed and fingertips steepled on the bridge of his nose. Samantha knew that pose. He was trying to stay in control.

"What's wrong?" Samantha demanded, suddenly sobered from the anesthesia. Flashes of memory returned, and her selfish plea rang through her mind. She attempted to sit up, but her lower abdomen was on fire. "Where's my baby? What happened?"

Ian startled, looking up and coming to stand by Samantha's bed. "You're awake," he said.

Samantha didn't comment on the obvious. She just

looked into his brown eyes, searching for confidence, something that would tell her everything was okay, but she saw a man who was afraid. "Ian," she said quietly. "Where is our baby?"

"She's in the NICU," Ian said. "She was born with a very low body temperature. The pediatric unit has hooked her up to a feeding tube, and she's under their heat lights." Ian's voice was steady, but Samantha could tell that was only for her benefit.

"I want to see her. I want to nurse her. She needs me right now." Samantha felt a pull toward her child that was fiercely territorial.

"Sam, she was airlifted to Pine View. They have the best NICU in the state. We can't see her right now." Ian put his hand on her arm. He could read the expression on her face, that stubborn, headstrong look she wore right before issuing some demand, solving a crisis. But damn it, Ian didn't want that part of her right now. He wanted some vulnerability—some softness that told him they were in this together.

No such luck.

"That's bullshit," Samantha said, pulling the IV out of her hands. "We need to be there. Let's go."

An alarm sounded, alerting the nursing staff that Samantha removed her IVs, and Ian stepped back from his wife as Roxanne ran into the room. When she saw Samantha struggling to get out of bed, she moved past Ian and put firm hands on her patient's shoulders.

"Sam, you just had major surgery," Roxanne said. "You need to stay here and rest for at least four days. Doctor's orders."

"She's not my doctor," Samantha retorted, pushing back

against Roxanne's hands. "My doctor would never agree to what's been done to me today. He would—"

"Dr. Soto saved you and our baby today," Ian cut Samantha off. "Rest for a little while. We'll see the baby as soon as we can."

"You go! What are you doing here? I'm fine! Go to the other hospital. Our baby needs to know that she hasn't been thrown away." Samantha pulled her blanket over her midsection, trying not to wince as her arm grazed her incision.

Ian paused for a moment, seething with anxiety and frustration. Sam had lost a great deal of blood, requiring a transfusion after her cesarean section, but she was still able to bark orders from her bed. While one part of him admired her for it, the other part wished he could shake her.

"What the hell are you waiting for?" Samantha yelled. "Go!"

Without a word, Ian walked out of the room, the unreality of the entire ordeal coming at him in waves. He passed Dr. Thompson in the hallway and didn't have the energy to do more than nod in passing.

"How are you feeling, Samantha?" Dr. Thompson asked as he approached her bed.

"Like I've just had a baby cut out of me and flown sixty miles away," Samantha snapped. "I've got to get out of here. She needs me. I can't stay in the hospital for four days. I was nursing Mitchell in my own bed at home this long after his delivery."

"I'll cut you a deal," Dr. Thompson said, leaning in. "If you'll consent to a stream of antibiotics in your IV to ward off infection, I'll let you go two days early."

Unnecessary antibiotics were something that Samantha hated even more than a cesarean section, but if it meant that she could get to her baby faster, she'd do it. She nodded, and Dr. Thompson made a note on the chart.

"You're a hell of a woman, Sam," he remarked, shaking his head and walking out of the room.

Two days later, Samantha wore a long summer dress under her coat for the ride to see her baby. She couldn't yet wear pants over her incision, so she was making do the best that she could. The radio was the only sound in the car while Samantha and Ian made their silent drive sixty miles east.

"Brrrrrr," the weatherman announced. "Wind chills expected to hit near twenty degrees tonight. Believe it or not, friends, today is the first day of spring. Those flowers are coming up under the snow this year."

"What do you know?" Samantha quietly asked Ian. He hadn't spoken to her much since their daughter was born, and while she assumed it was because he was as upset about the situation as she was, it went deeper. Samantha's treatment of everyone at the hospital, including Ian, had actually disgusted him. Instead of being grateful that these men and women had worked so quickly to save her and their tiny daughter's life, she was angry and talked down to them as if she knew better than they did.

"She can't latch onto a bottle," Ian said, ignoring Sam's soft comment about the weather. "So the NICU has inserted a feeding tube in hopes that she'll put on some weight. She doesn't squirm like the boys did, and I haven't heard her cry above a whimper. She seems pretty content, though, sleeping in the warming lights."

"Well, what's wrong with her?" Samantha pressed. "What's causing it, Ian?"

"I've just told you everything I know, Sam. I've only been able to hold her for short intervals. Otherwise, her body temperature drops too low—"

Samantha cut him off. "Well, did you try the kangaroo care that I recommended? She needs that skin-to-skin contact, Ian. It's all I've been able to tell you—"

"No, Samantha, I've been too busy trying to read our daughter's charts. The doctors know that I'm also an M.D., so they're not being too specific in her diagnosis. It's like they're afraid I'm going to work against them instead of with them."

Samantha turned to look out the window as they pulled into the parking lot at the hospital. Ian's frustration silenced her. He always wanted to fix everything, but he was quiet about it. They were polar opposites in that regard. She raised hell and he did research. Their differing approaches usually complemented each other, but now there was a tense distance between them.

At the hospital entrance, an orderly brought out a wheelchair for Samantha; they had been informed that she was coming and couldn't walk long distances yet. She sat in the chair in the lobby, waiting for Ian to park their car. In the moments she had to herself, she realized how nervous she was. The butterflies in her stomach were a new sensation to her; she wasn't even nervous on her wedding day. But now she was meeting her daughter for the first time—her daughter who was already three days old. This person with whom Samantha thought she would be so close—after all, she'd carried her as a part of her own body for nine months—was a stranger. On top of that, her daughter seemed to have some medical malady that no one could put a finger on. The past month had pushed Samantha to her limits, and now she was buzzing with nerves.

Ian walked through the automatic glass double doors, looking more like an undergraduate than a forty-year old psychiatrist. He was wearing a sweatshirt from his medical school and jeans that were tattered at the edges. His facial hair was closer to a beard than stubble. He gave Samantha a sad smile and took his position behind her. He pushed her into the elevator and then down a hall into a private room decorated with baby blue wallpaper and a foldout couch. A nurse from the NICU staff wheeled a plastic chamber into the room. "She's all yours. I'll be back for her in fifteen minutes to get her back under the lights." She turned to give the new family their privacy, but Samantha called out.

"Can I nurse her?" Samantha asked, getting situated on the couch beside the chamber. "My milk has come in. I've been pumping at the hospital, but my breasts are getting painful."

The nurse smiled. "She has a feeding tube in place now, but I don't see anything wrong with an attempt at a comfort nurse, for both of you."

Samantha nodded as the nurse quietly exited the room. As the door swung shut, she looked at the chamber instead of the baby. It reminded her of the glass coffin Sleeping Beauty slept in for so long. With a trembling exhale, she stuck her hands in the top to touch her baby's soft skin. She was tiny, smaller than either Luke or Mitch by a long shot. Samantha glanced at the identifying paperwork attached to the side of the chamber: "Baby Girl

Durkin. 5 lbs. 7 oz." Samantha was amazed that a full-term baby, and a third one at that, could be so small.

"She's miniature," Samantha breathed, almost to herself. She could sense Ian nodding beside her as she leaned into the case, pulling her daughter to her chest. She positioned her baby's head into the crook of her arm and pulled her breast from the top of the dress to nurse her. She gently held the baby to her chest but was surprised at the floppy mouth that met her skin. When Samantha was a child, she'd had a doll called a water baby—a rubber doll filled with warm water. Samantha couldn't believe how much her real daughter felt like that doll. She felt that she could do anything with the baby's body and she would get no resistance.

Samantha repositioned her child, trying to pull more of her own flesh into the baby's mouth, but her daughter didn't have the root reflex with which her boys had so greedily sought food. Samantha sighed. Of course, the baby wasn't able to nurse; she'd been separated from her mother for so long. The thought made Samantha furious. She wasn't even able to do the one thing she was sure would establish an intimate bond with her child. Closing her eyes, she tried to refocus her energy on the baby. She'd find a way to bond with her. It just might take awhile.

Pulling the baby into the crook of her arm as she readjusted her nursing bra, Samantha examined her girl's little face. Her daughter had almond-shaped eyes, and her mouth was slanted downward, as if she was a grumpy old man instead of a baby girl. When the baby opened her eyes, one eye seemed focused on her nose while the other seemed to be searching. There was no hint of the soulful staring her sons had done. Samantha's eyes filled with tears. Something wasn't right. It wasn't supposed to be like this.

"Ian," Samantha whispered. "She's not . . ." *Normal*, she almost finished but couldn't bear to say the word.

"Every symptom is nonspecific in her charts," Ian said, clearing his throat and trying to sound matter-of-fact. "I know they've ruled out Cerebral Palsy and Down's syndrome, but that's all I've got."

Samantha stroked her baby's cheek, feeling a surge of protectiveness for this infant who wouldn't even wrap her fingers around Samantha's pointer when she placed it in the palm of her hand.

"You know, she's three days old and she still doesn't have a name," Ian said to his wife.

Samantha looked up at Ian and then back into the little girl's face. She may not be able to make heads or tails of her child or the past week of hell that she and Ian had just survived, but she *could* feel the beauty and innocence radiating from her daughter. She was a strange angel, a flower growing beneath the snow. "Her name is Violet," Samantha whispered, smiling up at Ian. "She's our tiny, fragile flower—here to remind us that spring is just around the corner."

CHAPTER 2

"What is he talking about, Ian?" Samantha's impatient voice rang in Ian's ear as he tried to listen to the resident psychiatrist.

"Give us just a second, Sam." Ian managed to keep his voice calm in the chaos that surrounded him in the early morning emergency room. "Why don't you go sit down and I'll fill you in as soon as I know what's going on?"

Samantha gave her husband a look of contempt but walked away from him toward the waiting room.

"Basically, we have to keep her for forty-eight hours until she's had a full psych exam and we determine that she is no longer a threat to herself or to anyone else," Dr. Geller explained. Ian knew him mostly by reputation; he was a young doctor who was completing his residency in the emergency room.

"Look, I know that. I just want to make sure that when you're performing the evaluation, you understand that Violet has Prader-Willi Syndrome. She's different than other people, so you can't use the same baseline. I may sound like every other father with a neurotic teenage daughter, but I'm telling you: Violet *didn't* try to kill herself or even hurt herself tonight." Ian tried to maintain his professional demeanor, but he wanted to stress how important it was to take Violet's differences into consideration. "Dr. Alex Kraemer has been treating her since she hit puberty. He specializes in Prader-Willi, so his files would prove helpful in your own evaluation."

"Listen, Dr. Durkin, why don't you and I have a chat in my office? The waiting room is nowhere to have conversations like this." Dr. Geller motioned for Ian to follow him behind the heavy, secure doors that led to the emergency room staff offices. Ian waved Samantha over, and together they all walked into the small office. The room was tiny, and the couple felt claustrophobic with the grey walls and tile that surrounded them. Dr. Geller took a seat behind a simple plywood desk while Ian and Samantha sat across from him in black chairs with about half an inch of padding. Dr. Geller noticed Ian looking around his office and said dryly, "We don't all get to have a private practice, Dr. Durkin."

Ian knew that the other psychiatrist was trying to disarm him with humor, and he knew firsthand that psychiatrists weren't comedians who'd missed their calling in stand-up. It was a rookie mistake. Ian gave him a polite chuckle.

"So, why don't you tell me about Violet?" Dr. Geller smiled. His blond hair and dimples made him look more like a mischievous boy than a new doctor. He had delicate features that women probably either loved or envied, offset by a strong jawline and two rows of perfect, white teeth.

Samantha rolled her eyes. She'd been asked that question more times than she would have liked in her life, but Ian put a strong hand on her knee that said *Let me handle this.*

"Prader-Willi Syndrome is a complex and paradoxical disorder," Ian said. "Are you at all familiar with it?"

Dr. Geller shook his head. "I've heard of it, but it's not my specialty."

"Well, it's discovered by examining the chromosomes. Violet has a deletion in her fifteenth chromosome, which identifies the syndrome. There are physical characteristics, but as Violet has gotten older, we've seen more of the psychological and behavioral patterns come into play. Everything stems from the fact that there is a defect in Violet's hypothalamus: her brain is always telling her that she's starving to death. She is always in survival mode. Her food-related behaviors are the most significant: she hoards food, sneaks food, and steals food and money for food. She'll eat spoiled or frozen food, anything she can get her hands on. When Violet can't get to food, or her routine is disrupted in *any* way, we see characteristics of oppositional defiance. She will lie, manipulate, argue, or have a full-blown, lengthy tantrum. In addition to the outward symptoms we can all see, she has a sensitivity to stress and change. Her thought process is rigid, so she's unable to see things from other perspectives. She needs constant reassurance, which she gets through us, her therapists, and a set schedule that provides her with food security. Additionally, Violet suffers with an anxiety disorder, which only complicates her issues. She's currently on medication, monitored by Dr. Kraemer."

Dr. Geller nodded. "And what do you think got us here today?"

Samantha sat up straighter in her chair. "The past month has been a nightmare," she said quietly. "Violet is out of school right now, and she doesn't know what to do with herself anymore. I've been trying to get her settled into a routine at home. I even took two weeks off work before I started leaving her with a local college student during the day. Apparently it's not working, as we've had to . . ." She trailed off, her voice wrought with emotion.

"Violet can be very manipulative, but she wasn't trying to kill herself," Ian reiterated. "The only self-injurious behavior she's ever demonstrated is skin picking, and where there have been times in her life this was extremely severe, these days it typically only warrants some ointment and a bandage." Ian's voice broke, along with his professional resolve. This was his little girl, and whether or not she meant to kill herself, she'd managed to sneak past her sleeping father and hurt herself.

"I understand, Dr. Durkin." Dr. Geller's voice was low. "Listen, with Violet's disabilities, the state Department of Human Services is going to assign you a social worker." Dr. Geller could see Samantha's hackles rising and quickly added, "That person is here to help you—not judge you or Violet. He or she will work with you to determine your next steps when Violet is released from the hospital."

Samantha was defensive, not because she didn't want the help but because she was so relieved that she didn't have to ask for it. "How will that work?"

"I can't answer all the questions about that side of things, but she will be in touch with you soon. The social worker that the hospital works with most closely is Sheila Miren. I've worked with her many times, and I'm pretty sure she's who will be assigned your case. Her heart is in the right place. She works with families in crisis to find long-term solutions, but she won't force you to do anything. Remember, she's not the enemy."

Samantha was relieved by Dr. Geller's answer. "Can we see Violet now?" she asked.

"She's medicated, and I think it would be best if you didn't. This has been a traumatic experience for everyone, so I'd recommend getting some sleep, regrouping, and coming back tomorrow." Dr. Geller looked at the wall clock. It was eight a.m.

Ian stood and looked over to his wife, encouraging her to do the same. Samantha reluctantly followed. "Thank you so much. I anticipate hearing back from you soon?"

"You'll hear from Sheila, but my door is always open." Dr. Geller rose to shake the couple's hands and guide them back to the lobby.

Once they were back in the car, Samantha started to cry. Her sobs were sudden and uncontrollable. If she were in a different mindset, she'd feel shame for the raw emotion coursing through her, exposing her—but she was only relieved to release some of the terror that held her heart captive. Ian turned and wrapped his arms around his wife the best he could with the center console separating them.

"Sam, it's going to be okay. Violet is going to be fine," he whispered into his wife's ear. "We're all going to get the help we need."

Samantha looked up at him from behind the blonde hair that had fallen into her face. "This is terrible, but I'm almost relieved that no one can ignore this anymore. I don't know what I would do if she hurt herself more than she did, but now the world knows how messed up our lives are." Her head dropped back into her hands, where her sobs became more muffled but still filled the car with the pain of almost nineteen years of perceived failure.

Ian pulled away from Samantha and put his hands on the steering wheel. He took note of the blood that had started to dry on his shirt but then distracted himself by staring at the flowers that were in full bloom in the hospital parking lot. The sun was brilliant that morning, and the reflection of the rays off the delicate blossoms gave him something to focus on as he tried to make sense of this situation. Samantha's breakdown was completely out of character for her. She was so tough, while he was the sensitive one.

"I think I understand what you mean, Sam," Ian said, never taking his eyes off the flowers. When Samantha didn't respond, he shifted the car into reverse and headed back to their house.

· · ·

Samantha awoke disoriented in her king-sized bed, her eyes wide. She felt Ian's arms around her waist, and while it was comforting, it was unusual. The two hadn't slept together in a week; before that, they were usually on either side of the bed. She pulled her fingers from their interlacing position with his and rolled over. Ian grunted and rolled onto his back, and Samantha was relieved that she hadn't awakened him. The night before came back in brutal flashes: not knowing where Violet was, seeing her bloody in the bathroom, the ambulance ride where she could have sworn that the EMTs were judging her for her daughter's violent act against herself. Samantha didn't want to shake the terror that had accompanied the event; she felt as though she deserved to live in that awful space for the rest of her life. She'd failed her daughter, obviously. Healthy children didn't try to take their own lives. Healthy children had parents who preemptively acted on their behalf, preventing as much harm as they could.

Samantha rose and walked downstairs to make a pot of coffee. The clock indicated that it was five thirty in the afternoon, and she reconsidered introducing caffeine into her already late day. There were teabags in the pantry, and she turned to get the keys from her hiding spot, the fake drawer under the kitchen sink. They were missing. Dread filled Samantha's core. Violet must have gotten to them. Yet another failure on Samantha's part; she couldn't keep Violet safe in her own home. Her eyes welled again, but her chest ached from all the crying, so the tears just wearily rolled down her face as she sat on the couch and turned on the television.

She found a documentary on quantum physics, exploring string theory, and numbly watched it for almost an hour before the ringing phone brought her back to reality. She grabbed the cordless phone from her end table and answered.

"Sam, it's Alex Kraemer." Samantha recognized the warm voice on the other end of the line, and it was a simultaneous comfort and alert that she'd forgotten to call Violet's psychiatrist in the midst of the ruckus the night before.

"Oh, my God, Alex," Samantha cried. "I can't believe I didn't call you. Do you know what's going on?"

"I do. I've been in communication with Michael Geller at the hospital. It's okay that you didn't call me. You had enough going on." Dr. Kraemer's voice was salve to the wounds that had been rubbed raw. "Is Ian around? I'd like to talk with you both."

"He's sleeping—something neither of us has done in a while. I don't want to wake him, but I need to know what's going on."

Dr. Kraemer cleared his throat. "Well, Violet is fine, medically. She isn't going to sustain any long-term injuries, aside from some pretty nasty scars on her arm. I'm calling because the blood work that the hospital ran indicated that her system was completely clear of any drugs."

Samantha was puzzled. "Of course it was. Violet is sneaky, but I don't think she's ever had a drug problem."

"Samantha, I mean completely clear. No trace of her medications for anxiety or depression. Have you been giving her the medication that she's prescribed?"

"Yes! I give it all to her right after she has her breakfast. Things are under such lock and key around here that I know she gets her medicine every morning. It just doesn't make any sense . . ." Samantha trailed off, perplexed by the news that her daughter's psychiatrist was delivering. Of course, Violet's behavior for the past week made more sense if she was without her medication for her anxiety disorder.

"We both know that Violet has a tendency to be manipulative. Can you be sure that she is actually taking the medication that you're administering?" Dr. Kraemer asked.

Samantha tapped her fingers on the end table. She saw Violet swallow the pills with her milk or juice from breakfast each morning . . . or did she? There was always a chance that Violet was lying. "If you're asking if I physically inspect her mouth each morning, the answer is no."

Dr. Kraemer sighed. "I should have told you to try that. With Violet's recent transitions—being out of school, staying home during the day—it's not surprising that she's acting out. But more than that, I think Violet has not been taking her meds."

Samantha's heart sank. All of this could have been prevented. "I'm so sorry," was all that she could muster.

"Don't hold yourself responsible. Based on her evaluation from Dr. Geller and her clinical file, we're recommending that she be held in the psychiatric ward of the hospital for two weeks. That will give us plenty of time to get her medication regulated again. I am going to work with the head of the psychiatric unit, explaining Violet's particular needs for food security and managed portions. I think we'll see a drastic improvement in her in that time. Her dependency and need for reassurance will kick in staying in a new place, but ultimately, it's the best thing for her right now."

Samantha nodded before realizing that Dr. Kraemer couldn't see her. "Okay. Do we need to do anything?"

"Since you're her legal guardians, I'll need your signatures on the admissions paperwork. Otherwise, and this is just a personal recommendation, I think that you and Ian could benefit from some therapy yourselves. It's been an intense two weeks around your house."

"Well, you've got that right," Samantha said. "Ian is sleeping, but as soon as he wakes, I'll fill him in. We'll go to the hospital first thing tomorrow morning."

"Great. I also know that your case has been turned over to Sheila Miren, a social worker with the state. She's wonderful; I've worked with her before. She may also want to meet with you tomorrow to discuss Violet's treatment in the hospital and your next steps for her release." Dr. Kraemer's voice was reassuring, but it just twisted the knife in Samantha's heart. Her daughter was being admitted to a psychiatric hospital. She needed a social worker to help get her family's affairs in order. As many times as Samantha perceived that she'd failed Violet in the past, this was by far the most helpless she'd ever felt.

"Thanks for everything, Alex. We'll be in touch soon," Samantha said, hanging up the phone.

"Who was that?" Ian sleepily asked from behind her.

"Alex. He was calling with an update," Samantha said, looking back to her husband. His dark hair was ruffled from sleep, and he rubbed his eyes and stretched.

"What's going on?" Ian was immediately awake. He moved to the couch and took a seat next to Samantha.

"Violet didn't have any of her medication in her system. Apparently, she hasn't been taking it, although I can guarantee that I've been giving it to her every day. Alex recommended that she be admitted to the hospital for two weeks of intensive therapy and to get her medication regulated. We officially have a 'case' with the state and we can expect a call from a social worker to set up a meeting for tomorrow. We have to sign the admissions paperwork tomorrow." Samantha went through the list of major topics that she and Dr. Kraemer had covered.

"That all sounds about right," Ian said, shaking his head. He was familiar with these cases, but he never thought he'd live the experience on the other side of the desk.

Just then, the phone rang again. Ian got the cordless phone from his wife's lap and answered. She'd just been overloaded with information, and he would take care of whoever was calling with news now.

"Is this Dr. Durkin? My name is Sheila Miren, with the state." The voice on the other end of the line was that of a young woman.

"Social worker," Ian mouthed to Samantha, who was looking at him quizzically.

"Yes, this is Dr. Durkin. Hi, Sheila."

"I'm calling to set an appointment with you and your wife regarding Violet's care. Have you spoken with Dr. Kraemer?"

"My wife just got off the phone with him. We'll be at the hospital to sign Violet's admission paperwork tomorrow," Ian said, raising an eyebrow at his wife in hopes that he got the timeline right.

"Great. Would you be available to meet there tomorrow morning? Say around ten a.m.?"

"Sure," Ian said. "That will give us time to visit with Violet before our meeting."

Samantha jumped up and grabbed a pen to write down the schedule for the following day.

"We'll chat then," Sheila said. "Take care, Dr. Durkin."

"You, too," Ian said, trying to make his voice smile despite the ache in his chest. He hit the end button and took a deep breath. Samantha had returned to her seat beside him, and he looked over at her. "I think there might be a light at the end of this tunnel. I just hope it isn't a freight train."

CHAPTER 3

"Could we just lay the stakes a little closer to the fence? I don't want any of the kids to bounce out onto the porch." Samantha shook her head at the men who were installing the bounce house. The pink and purple castle had taken up most of the yard behind their century-old Lincoln Park brownstone. Samantha wanted to make sure that everything was just so—her daughter's life so far had been challenging, and the little girl deserved a wonderful time for her fifth birthday. The week before, Violet had been fitted with little glasses, a victory considering the three surgeries to correct her astigmatism and the lack of muscle control in her eyes.

"That looks great, guys. Thank you so much," Samantha called out as she went back into her house. She scanned the bar top in the den, where the food was carefully positioned for guests to build their own plates. She stopped short on the second sandwich tray, where she noticed that about a third of the sandwiches were missing.

"Lukas! Mitchell!" Samantha yelled at the bottom of the stairs.

Her sons clambered down the stairs, Mitchell in the front and Lukas clumsily tripping over his feet on the last step.

"What's up, Mom?" Mitchell asked.

"Exactly what were you two thinking? Those sandwiches are for the party!"

Both boys looked up her at innocently.

"What sandwiches, Mom?" Lukas asked.

"These." Samantha motioned to the tray along the bar, the Saran Wrap messily balled to the center.

"Mom, we've been upstairs playing Sega the whole time," Mitchell said.

"Yeah right, Sega with a snack, huh? You boys know better than to lie. You . . ." Samantha trailed off as Ian appeared at the top of the stairs.

"Hey, guys, Sonic's waiting for us. What's going on, Sam?"

"The boys." Samantha pursed her lips together. "They ate almost half the sandwiches from one of the trays."

"No, they didn't. They've been upstairs playing video games with me," Ian said, his brow furrowing in confusion. "We've been up there for the better part of an hour, ever since the catering company dropped off all the food. I thought if you had Violet, I could get them out of your hair while you set up."

Samantha looked around. Where was Violet? She'd gotten so caught up in the party, with the inflatables company and the catering showing up at almost the same time, that she assumed Ian was keeping an eye on her.

"Go back upstairs, boys. I'm so sorry that I yelled at you," Samantha said as she turned to walk back into the kitchen. Ever since last Christmas, when Violet had crawled on top of the fridge with her brothers' stocking candy, that was the first place Samantha looked when she couldn't immediately find her. Sure enough, Violet was there, her chubby hands stuffing a whole turkey sandwich into her mouth.

"Violet! Come down here, right now!" Samantha said, frowning as her daughter's round belly heaved with a gasp for air. She'd been eating so fast that she forgot to breathe. "Violet!" Samantha said again. "If you don't come down, you're going to spend the afternoon in your room while the party is going on."

Violet looked down at her mother and stuck out her tongue. Chewed bread gave it a sickly, white appearance.

"That's not what we do when we're asked something," Samantha said, already on the barstool so she could reach her daughter.

"Hate Mommy!" Violet screamed. Her wails quickly filled the kitchen with the sound of abject despair. The cries became muffled as she shoved another whole sandwich in her mouth. The crying and eating at the same time made for a terrible combination, and soon Violet gagged, her eyes bulging. Samantha reached Violet just as the food that was stuck in her throat came back up and she spit it down on her mother. Samantha's arms were covered with half-chewed cold cuts and sticky bits of bread. Reflexively, Samantha pulled away, and the bar stool came toppling down with her. More stunned than hurt, Samantha rose to her feet again. Violet looked down at her mother from her perch and gave a warrior's yell before jumping off the refrigerator, her knees smacking the cold ceramic tile with a bony crack.

"Vi! Oh, my God!" Samantha stooped to her daughter, but before she could reach her, Violet bounded away and up the stairs with a banshee's screech and a slight limp. Her door slammed moments later.

Samantha looked down at her food-covered shirt before glancing over at the clock on her stove. Guests would be arriving in twenty minutes. Needing a moment to herself, she washed her hands and arms in the kitchen sink and then walked upstairs, trying to calm herself with every step. Her boys had never pulled anything like this, and as she often felt with Violet, she wasn't sure if she should comfort her or discipline her. Instead, she decided to change her shirt before coming back down the hallway and trying Violet's bedroom door. It was locked.

In Lukas's bedroom, Samantha asked Ian to step outside and speak with her. After she explained what happened, Ian spoke. "Oh, my God, Samantha, is Violet okay?"

"I would assume so, since she ran up the stairs, but I don't know. She's locked me out," Samantha said, keeping a measure of control in her tone. She was trying to discuss their daughter's out-of-control behavior, and he, like always, was thinking about something completely different.

"Did you even try to get in?" Ian asked, looking at Samantha as if he didn't even know her.

"We have guests arriving . . ." Samantha started, before Ian interrupted her.

"To hell with the guests. They're arriving because it's Violet's birthday." Ian stomped off to the master bathroom, then back past Samantha in the hallway carrying a box of bandages and a bottle of hydrogen peroxide. Samantha watched as he knocked on Violet's door, and said, "Vi, it's Daddy. I want to take care of you." The door clicked and slowly opened, and Ian disappeared inside.

Samantha composed herself and went downstairs. She took a deep breath, unwrapped the party trays, turned on the stereo, and poured herself a glass of wine. Just as she sat down for a moment, the doorbell rang. Samantha stood, smiled, and greeted her first guests. They dropped Violet's gift at the table in the dining room, and as Samantha was trying to fabricate a reason Violet wasn't downstairs, her daughter appeared at the foot of the stairs, all smiles. Her tear-stained face, the bandages on her knees, and a slight limp were the only indication that anything was out of the ordinary.

"Birthday girl had a little spill, but Daddy got her all better," Ian said to their guests, smiling. Samantha was disgusted. He always wanted to pretend that everything was okay and that Violet was fine, if a little slower to develop than her brothers.

"Vi's birthday!" Violet gushed to her cousins. "See my cool goggles?" She pointed out the small purple frames on her face.

...

"Violet, it's time for your cake, sweetheart," Samantha called out into the backyard where Violet was playing with her cousins and friends from the daycare she attended. As soon as she heard the word *cake*, Violet bounded from the bounce house and landed on her feet. Samantha noticed that her daughter was hobbling, and her eyes widened when she saw that Violet's ankle was swollen to twice its normal size. The strap on the Mary Jane shoes that her daughter was wearing was barely visible beneath the skin that was starting to touch over the top.

"Violet! Your foot!" Samantha exclaimed, scooping her daughter in her arms and taking a seat on a patio chair to pull off her shoe. After a short struggle, and with a captive audience of parents and family members, Samantha found that not only was Violet's ankle swollen, she had bruising from her lower calf extending to the top of her foot.

"Will someone please get my husband?" Samantha asked, giving the crowd a reason to disburse. She turned her attention to her daughter again.

"Violet, did you hurt your foot in the bounce house? Why didn't you come get Mommy?" Samantha's eyes were concerned as she focused on the tiny freckles beneath Violet's green eyes.

"Cake, Mommy!" Violet demanded, not giving a second thought to her foot.

"Violet, you're hurt. We have to figure out what's wrong with you before we have our cake," Samantha said, looking around for Ian.

Violet struggled to get out of her mother's arms. "Cake, Mommy! Now!" she screamed, pushing against her mother's grip.

"Not now, Violet. Wait for Daddy," Samantha was losing patience. And where was Ian anyway?

"Cake! Now!" Violet roared. Then she screamed with more power than could possibly be contained in such a little body.

"Stop it, Violet," Samantha whispered, hoping to diffuse the situation by lowering her voice.

Violet squirmed in Samantha's arms until she was facing her mother. Then she lifted her hand back and slapped Samantha across the cheek. Stunned, Samantha let go of Violet, and the girl fell to the floor. She picked herself up and made a hobbling beeline for the living room, where all the guests had assembled for the birthday song. Samantha got up and chased her daughter, shocked that she'd just been slapped and that Violet could run on that ankle.

"Ian," she called out. "Could you get Violet? She's clearly hurt her foot."

Ian hadn't received the message that Samantha needed him and was making his way through the crowd to see what she was talking about when all the guests at the party burst into laughter at the same time. Both parents turned to see what was so funny, and they realized that Violet had stuck both hands into the cake and was eating it greedily.

Since Ian was closer, he picked up his daughter around the waist and held her so that he could look at the foot Samantha was claiming to be injured. He was shocked when he saw the swollen purple mess at the end of his daughter's leg. Violet cried out, loudly, as soon as her hands lost contact with the confection.

"Thank you to everyone for coming, but I'm afraid we're going to have to cut the party short, as Violet's hurt herself and it looks like a visit to the emergency room is in order." Ian talked over his daughter's cries with a smile, trying to make light of the situation but knowing that his daughter's ankle was broken.

...

Samantha slid Violet into her bed at one a.m. They were lucky there wasn't much of a wait at the emergency room and the doctors were able to set Violet's ankle in-house and get her home. She was fine except for the broken bone, and the doctors kept commenting on how they'd never seen a kid with a broken bone act so coolly about it all. Samantha was relieved when Violet passed out in her car seat, her soft snoring the only noise as the family made their way back home. When they arrived at their brownstone, Samantha carefully slid the child out of her car seat restraints, carried her inside and up the stairs, and tucked her into the bed without waking her. Thankfully, Ian's parents had been at the party and took the boys home with them so that both parents could be with Violet at the hospital.

Downstairs, Samantha found Ian picking up the remnants of the birthday party. She pitched in, gathering all the trash that was to be delivered to the dumpster, and the two of them worked in silence until Samantha just couldn't stand it anymore.

"I didn't know she was hurt, Ian," she said, placing her hands on her hips. Her voice was desperate for some acknowledgment that Violet's injury wasn't her fault. "She played just fine until I noticed it."

"I know, Sam," Ian responded. "I didn't, either. I just don't understand what happened. Did she break her ankle jumping from the refrigerator? Or did she do something wacky in the bounce house? I guess we'll never know, since she gave no indication of any pain, ever."

"Ian, something isn't *right*," Samantha said, giving voice to the fear that crept quietly along the sidelines of her every thought. "No child breaks a bone without any reaction. What can we do? Should I take this to the pediatrician?"

Ian stopped working and looked at his wife. She was so earnest in her attempts to "make things right," but she felt powerless to fix things. He knew that she was frustrated, but he was, too. "Sam, Dr. Peterson hasn't had any ideas about what's going on with Violet so far. What makes you think that he'll know what this means?"

"At least he'll have record of everything. That way, when we do figure out what's going on, we'll have documented evidence to support whatever claim, or diagnosis, or whatever it is that we're in search of." Samantha straightened. Even though things looked bleak, she refused to give up hope that they would find the missing pieces that made Violet's picture complete.

· · ·

The next week, Samantha was getting ready to take Violet to the pediatrician. It was his first appointment of the day, so Samantha could still come into work for the afternoon. Ian had already taken the boys to school, and Samantha put on the coffee pot so that she could have her cup to go. She left Violet watching *Sesame Street* on the couch while she ran upstairs to grab a pair of earrings.

When she came back downstairs, Violet was missing from the couch.

"Vi, where are you, baby?" Samantha called out. Silence. Samantha looked toward the top of the refrigerator before remembering that Violet was in an ankle cast and couldn't climb very well. She heard a rustling in the pantry, walked over, and opened the door.

Violet was sitting with her legs straight out in the middle of the pantry, smiling at her mother through the now open door. A brown mess covered her face and shirt.

"Violet, what do you have everywhere?" Samantha gasped.

"Cookies, Mommy."

Samantha came into the pantry and helped her daughter up to see what was covering her. The creamy substance was smeared up the girl's arms, caked in between her fingers, and almost rubbed into her cheeks. She decided to be brave and smell it, just to see. As she moved her nose towards the girl, she sighed in relief.

"Violet, that was the chocolate icing for the cupcakes we were going to bake for Mitchell's class," Samantha said, exasperated.

Violet just smiled at her mother, and Samantha saw the empty containers that were hidden behind her little girl.

"Vi, it's *all* gone. There were three containers of frosting in here. Did you—" Samantha couldn't bring herself to think that her five-year-old had eaten three entire containers of chocolate frosting.

"Violet, you're going to get sick!" Samantha exclaimed, picking up her child. Just then, Violet's face paled. Her stomach gave a peculiar gurgle, and Samantha's arms were suddenly covered in another warm, sticky substance. Samantha closed her eyes, trying to collect herself. Of course, Violet would have an episode of explosive diarrhea while she was in an ankle cast, while Samantha was holding her, and just before Samantha had to take her to the doctor's office.

"Come on, baby. Let's get cleaned up." Samantha carried her daughter into the master bedroom. She quickly ran a bath, changed her clothes, and scrubbed her hands and arms in the sink. Once she was clean, she called the office and let them know she was staying home with Violet that day. She hung up and inspected Violet's cast. She thanked her lucky stars that Violet was still in training pants and found the cast miraculously clean, tying a plastic bag around it to prevent it getting wet in the bath.

Filling a cup with the warm water from the bath, Samantha carefully poured it over her daughter's fine hair. She watched as the water moved down her chubby arms. Samantha had called her boys "Michelin Men," with rolls on their arms and legs that resembled the character made of tires, but her boys had lost their rolls when they started walking. Violet had been a tiny baby. She'd had no suck reflex and couldn't breastfeed, nor could she take a regular bottle of formula. Samantha and Ian had needed to find a special, modified nipple for the bottle so that their youngest could eat at all. Now, Violet was five and her skin buckled in rings up her arms and on her thighs. When Samantha considered all the things that were different about Violet's childhood than her brothers', it overwhelmed her. She hoped that the broken bone and binge eating might be the clues that the pediatrician had been missing.

Samantha pulled Violet from the bathtub into her lap and wrapped her in a plush, green towel, pulling it over her head to dry her hair. She rubbed hard and then opened it to reveal her face. Samantha reached down and gave her little girl Eskimo kisses, and they both giggled. After getting her dressed, Samantha slid her into the car seat and headed to the doctor's office. Even with their delay, they wouldn't be more than a few minutes late. She wasn't even sure what she'd say. Dr. Peterson, the same doctor who'd treated Luke and Mitch, didn't seem to take her seriously anymore. She didn't care if she annoyed him, though; she was going to get her daughter the help she obviously needed.

...

Samantha carefully sat Violet on the examination table and stood in front of her, reading a book about a little piggy princess. Violet giggled every time Samantha snorted for the character.

"Hello, ladies." Dr. Peterson entered the small examination room with his gaze on Violet's chart. His blue eyes and grey hair contrasted with his tan skin, and he looked up over his thin wire-rimmed glasses at Violet. "I see that we have an upset tummy, Miss Violet. Oh, and a broken ankle to boot." He laughed at his own joke before moving over to Violet with a thermometer.

Violet looked up at the doctor, her green eyes filled with fear. She glanced over to her mother, who smiled reassuringly.

"Her upset stomach seems to have passed now," Samantha said. "She was only sick once today, and it was after she ate a lot of frosting. Besides, that's not why we're here."

"How much is a lot?" Dr. Peterson raised one of his eyebrows, ignoring Samantha's last statement.

"Three containers," Samantha said, looking the doctor straight in the eye.

"Well, she doesn't have a fever, and she seems to be acting normally," Dr. Peterson said. "So she had violent diarrhea after she ate three containers of frosting? I can imagine so!" He chuckled.

"Dr. Peterson, as you know, Violet is my third child. I'm no stranger to toddlers doing strange things. She broke her ankle at her birthday party. It's fractured in four places, but she gave no indication that anything was wrong. We don't even know when it got broken. The only time she ever cries or does much of anything is when we deny her food, and speaking of that—*three* containers of frosting? She was left alone for fewer than ten minutes, just enough time for me to run upstairs and finish getting ready. When I came downstairs, I found her hiding in the pantry, covered in the stuff. She sneaks food into her bedroom. She ate half a party tray of subs at her birthday party. She has to sit next to her preschool teacher during lunch, or she'll steal food out of the other kids' hands! I'm truly at a loss."

Dr. Peterson flipped back through Violet's chart. "It seems, Mrs. Durkin, that you have a tough girl who likes to eat. A little girl who is the only girl, and the youngest child, and is maybe used to getting her own way?"

Samantha pursed her lips together. She didn't like the doctor's implication that Violet's behavior was her fault. "Dr. Peterson, everyone likes to eat. Our family is composed of big food lovers, but Violet acts as though she's *never* fed. The ideas that she has about food have never occurred to me, nor to anyone that I've *ever* seen. And the pain . . . it's like she's a robot whose only mission is to seek food. She acts like she's trapped on a desert island and will run on a broken ankle to get to her next meal. Literally."

"Samantha, you're a working mother. You might feel guilt at not being at home with your child as much as you'd like, especially with Violet. She's had so many health problems, and your delivery was so traumatic for both of you. You also know that she's your baby, so when she's grown, you're done with this stage of life. She can feel your anxiety, and she's acting out."

Samantha was appalled. "So you're saying that I don't watch my child, and that she acts out because *I'm* a nutcase? Really? I'm bringing my daughter to see you because she has real medical problems, and you call yourself a real medical professional. If you're going to tell me that my daughter's problems are a result of my indulging her, I'm going to find a doctor who will listen to what's going on and not cast aspersions on me for being a working mother."

"That's not what I'm saying, Samantha." Dr. Peterson tried to calm her. "I'm just saying that we should try some simple approaches before we jump to any medical conclusions. Why don't you try to enroll her in a dance class? She could get more activity and it would be something that the two of you could do together. Try to have all your meals with her—"

Samantha didn't let him finish before she collected her daughter and her bag and walked out of his office. She strapped Violet into her car seat, walked calmly to the driver's seat, and burst into tears.

"You're okay, Mama," Violet's voice carried from the back seat. "I love you."

The sound of her daughter using the same words that Samantha used to comfort her made Samantha's tears fall even heavier.

"I know, baby. I love you, too." Samantha tried to collect herself and dialed her husband's phone number.

"Dr. Durkin," he answered.

"It's me," Samantha said. "Violet ate three canisters of chocolate frosting before we even went to the doctor. She had an accident that covered both of us. I took her to the doctor, who said she's feeding off my anxiety and acting out. She didn't react to her broken bone because she has two rough older brothers. I was furious. I fired our pediatrician. We have to find a new one."

"Wait. Sam, slow down. What happened, exactly?" Ian's voice was confused but patient. Samantha could picture him furrowing his brow, trying to follow.

She took a deep breath and told the story again, slowly.

"Do you think I did the right thing?" Samantha asked her husband.

"Damn right, you did. I can't believe he would attack your parenting when you were coming to him for answers. We've been seeing him for seven years." Ian's voice was thick with anger.

"I know. Ian, I just don't know what else to do."

"You're not the only one, Sam." Ian sighed. "I love you."

"Love you, too. I'm keeping Violet home today. I'll try to get some work done this afternoon when Sue brings the boys home."

"Sounds good. I'll see you as soon as I can." Ian's voice was resigned. This was just what they all needed.

...

Three months, six pediatrician's interviews, and no luck later, Ian made it his mission to find diagnostic testing options, something that would give him some indication of what could be going on with Violet. Each evening, he pored over every medical journal he could find. He searched for each of Violet's symptoms: her high tolerance for pain, insatiable appetite, even the feeding problems and lack of mobility as an infant. He was starting to bang his head against the wall. All the while, the intensity and frequency of Violet's behaviors were increasing.

Samantha had to buy their five-year-old clothes in a much larger size. Violet's jean legs were rolled around her ankles so that she didn't trip over the pants that were snug on her waist but dragged the ground. Neither parent could pinpoint a reason for the weight gain. They occasionally allowed her a treat, but she ate the same portions as the rest of the family at the dinner table.

Finally, late one night, Ian was scouring an online journal when he saw a story that intrigued him. There was a new genetic panel called a FISH test that covered a number of genetic disorders that were previously untraceable. The test could be used to find the likelihood of cancerous cells forming, but University Hospital was running the panel for patients at birth who were showing mild or insidious symptoms but for whom no diagnosis was easily found. Ian printed the article and brought it out to the living room, where Samantha was curled up with a book.

"Sam, read this!" Ian thrust the paper at her.

"What is it?" Samantha looked up at her husband, lowering her reading glasses.

"It's an article about a genetic panel that doctors are now running at University Hospital."

"A genetic panel? Like the amnio? Didn't we have one of those when she was born, to rule out Down's syndrome?"

"We did, but this one covers more ground. It's called a FISH test—fluorescence in situ hybridization. Basically, it checks the entire DNA for any errors or abnormalities. I think that could bring us a step closer to figuring out what's going on with Violet." Ian sat next to Samantha on the couch, his chest about to burst with excitement—there were no guarantees, but at least he'd found something.

"Let's give it a shot. University Hospital hasn't been able to diagnose her with any other test. What's the worst thing that could happen? We still won't know what's wrong with her?" Samantha gave a cold chuckle at her last bit of dark humor.

...

Two months later, Samantha and Ian sat in the office of Dr. Jean Howie, a geneticist. Her office at the hospital was just as sterile as an operating room. In contrast to Ian's office of rich mahogany, this one was furnished with black chairs with minimal padding, surrounded by white tile and a distinctly medicinal smell. Dr. Howie got Violet in for a FISH test a few weeks before, and when she called to meet with Ian and Samantha, they were convinced that maybe they'd finally get some answers.

"Ian, Samantha, we ran the panel on Violet, and we found an absence of genetic material in the typically active fifteenth chromosome." Dr. Howie delivered the news so casually that Samantha had to take a moment to process that her daughter had just been given a diagnosis.

"What does that mean?" Samantha asked. She looked over at Ian, whose brow furrowed in concentration—or in preparation for the news that was coming.

"The deletion of this paternally-delivered chromosome is consistent with Prader-Willi Syndrome," Dr. Howie explained. "Looking over Violet's medical history, we believe her symptoms to be consistent with the syndrome as well."

"What the hell is Prader-Willi Syndrome?" Samantha asked. She turned to Ian and then back to Dr. Howie. "Will you translate, please?"

"Prader-Willi Syndrome," Dr. Howie said, "is very rare, with incidences only as high as maybe one in every fifteen thousand births. Most doctors and pediatricians have never even heard of the syndrome, much less know how to treat it. The only way of discovering it is through the genetic panel," she added, with no small amount of pride.

"That's really interesting, Doctor," Samantha said in a clipped tone. "But what is Prader-Willi? What are we in for?"

Dr. Howie passed them a sheaf of paperwork, mostly printed articles. "Read over these pieces when you have time," she said. "As for additional support, your best bet would be to contact an organization called Prader-Willi Syndrome Association USA, or PWSA-USA. We also have pediatricians and nutritionists on staff who will work with you and Violet to help her live a healthy and happy life. All of their information is included in that paperwork."

"Okay, wait," Ian finally spoke up. "We'll read this, but Jesus—at least explain the diagnosis first."

Dr. Howie sighed. Then, almost too slowly, she said, "Prader-Willi Syndrome is inherited from the parents. Every human has twenty-three chromosomes. In cases of Prader-Willi Syndrome, we look for abnormalities of the fifteenth chromosome. Three main genetic errors can occur on the fifteenth chromosome that result in Prader-Willi Syndrome. Seventy percent or more result from a deletion in the fifteenth chromosome donated by the father—a deletion means some genetic information is missing. Twenty-five percent result from maternal uniparental disomy, which means that there are two

44

fifteenth chromosomes from the mother and none from the father. Two to five percent have an error in the 'imprinting' process that renders the father's chromosome nonfunctional, so it is 'tossed out.' In Violet's case, the FISH test confirmed she is in the first category—she is missing information from Ian's chromosome.

"The syndrome was discovered in the 1950s. Characteristics are hypotonia, or low muscle development, especially in infants, and failure to thrive as a child, followed by a voracious appetite. Food hoarding, stealing—anything that can be done to get food will happen. The hypothalamus—the center of the brain that controls hunger, metabolism, body temperature, and other systems—does not work the same way in people with this syndrome, so patients with Prader-Willi always feel as though they are about to starve to death. They never feel satiated. They are in a constant drive state."

"Drive state," Samantha said quietly, thinking back to her daughter running on a broken ankle to get to her birthday cake. The girl who stole food from her classmates at preschool . . . The girl who would do anything to finally feel satiated . . .

"Yes, the syndrome is paradoxical, though. In addition to the greatly increased appetite, the metabolism is affected, causing patients to burn calories at about a third of the rate of a normal metabolism. In order for Violet to thrive, we need to focus primarily on her food consumption and activity levels. If Violet's food consumption isn't strictly monitored, she could literally eat herself to death or suffer from many of the long-term complications of severe obesity—cardiopulmonary problems, diabetes. It may sound drastic, but parents with children with this syndrome typically lock up any food in their homes. With a strict schedule for meal time and diet management, you'll find that Violet will be much healthier and happier."

"Dr. Howie, I think I understand what you're saying, but what does this mean for the long term? What can we anticipate as she gets older?" Samantha asked.

A flicker of unease passed over Dr. Howie's face. "Well, like I said, rigid structure around her access to food will be imperative. I can't emphasize that enough. In some cases, people with Prader-Willi will eat any sort of food item that they can get their hands on. I mean *any*— spoiled food from the trash, coffee grounds, eggshells."

"Well that's enough to make anyone sick," Samantha said, looking bewildered. "Wouldn't we notice if she was doing that? She's never eaten enough to vomit, and I'm certain that we'd know if she was eating trash—it would make her violently ill."

"Not always," Dr. Howie said. "You've never seen your daughter vomit because most people with Prader-Willi Syndrome have distinctive neurological features, one of which is the lack of the vomiting reflex."

Samantha and Ian sat in stunned silence.

Dr. Howie continued. "Beyond that, Prader-Willi patients typically have moderate to severe learning disabilities, with their IQ level falling anywhere between twenty and ninety. You'll need to work with the school district to get Violet evaluated. She should qualify for special education services because of the syndrome. The school district will work with you to put together an Individualized Education Plan, or IEP. You took Violet to the pediatrician in part because she doesn't seem to register pain the way your other children do—that's another characteristic of Prader-Willi. She might develop obsessive-compulsive behaviors, like repeatedly picking her skin, pulling her hair, or obsessing on certain topics or objects. Many people with this syndrome will suffer with co-occurring psychiatric conditions, particularly OCD, depression, and anxiety disorders, as they get older. We don't typically see them reach full sexual maturity. As for the rest of the aging process, unfortunately we don't have a lot of information. We used to see an average lifespan of maybe twenty, twenty-five years. However," Dr. Howie added, seeing the crushed looks on Samantha and Ian's faces, "we are seeing patients live much longer, since we know more about the syndrome and are better able to provide treatment, sometimes in twenty-four-hour therapeutic residential care."

Samantha's stomach churned as she listened, overwhelmed at what she was hearing. For a moment, she wished fiercely for ignorance again, for a time when she could invent some benign reason for why her little girl ate so much or wasn't developing the way her brothers had. An average lifespan of twenty or twenty-five years? Even if there had been advances, it horrified Samantha to think that not long ago, Violet's prognosis would have been so grim. As it was, residential care? No. That was impossible. Ian took her hand, and she gripped it almost too tightly. Because she couldn't articulate her fear, she crisply changed the subject. "And what is the treatment? I mean, you mentioned locking away food, which we can do at home, but what about Violet's school? She's there five days a week, and she has regular lunchtime. We'll need to—"

"The school should be flexible to meet Violet's needs, especially if she can access special education and related services and if those are specified in her IEP," Ian interrupted, and then took a deep breath. Violet. His baby. He couldn't yet imagine the changes they would need to make in their lives, but he was willing to do whatever it took to keep Violet healthy. He wanted to start now.

"Thank you." Ian stood to shake the other doctor's hand. "We'll be in touch with the contacts you've listed here. We can't tell you how glad we are to at least have an answer."

Once the Durkins were back in their car, Samantha realized that neither of them had said a word to the other since Dr. Howie had given them the diagnosis they'd been seeking.

"How are you doing?" she asked, putting her hand on Ian's forearm as he pulled out of the parking spot.

"I'm still in shock," Ian replied. "I mean, all of those symptoms that seemed so disconnected . . . the lack of muscle development when she was a baby, the appetite, the high pain tolerance . . . we've been searching for this diagnosis for so long, but I feel like we have more questions than answers."

"I know," Samantha sighed, looking out the window. "I'm relieved in one sense that there is a name for all of Violet's issues, but I've never even *heard* of Prader-Willi. I'm terrified that her life won't get any better just because we know what to call it."

"The only thing we can do now is what Dr. Howie told us to do," Ian said firmly. "Let's make a stop at the hardware store and get our reconstruction process underway. After the kids are in bed tonight, we'll make a schedule and get together some paperwork for Violet's school."

Samantha and Ian arrived home around three p.m. Ian pulled into their garage, and Samantha grabbed the two large bags from the trunk. Since Violet was already with Sue, their babysitter, the couple got to work on the kitchen for the new life they would have to undertake with Violet. Without another word, Samantha removed the cabinet knobs while Ian fired up the drill and read the instructions for installation. After working silently for about an hour, Samantha finally spoke. "Remember our first house? When we decided to decorate everything ourselves?"

"Decorate? You wanted me to turn into a master carpenter." Ian didn't look up from his project.

Samantha laughed. "I did not. I just wanted simple paint and some hardwood floors. You were the one who decided that we needed a bar off the kitchen."

Ian smiled at the memory. He was completing his residency at a local hospital and nursing home. Samantha had just moved to the Midwest from Cambridge, having just finished business school. They bought a small house, about a thousand square feet, just to get them through for a few years. Although it was nothing compared to where they currently lived, they were so proud to own something.

"This is kind of like that, right? Doing something that seems unnecessary to everyone else—but going forward anyway." Samantha smiled at their innocence then.

"I guess," Ian said. He appreciated Samantha's efforts to make him feel better. And while he was the one who had initiated this action, now that he was home, he'd rather just take a cup of hot tea on the porch and mourn the things he may never get to do with his daughter. She had a lifelong condition that would require constant supervision. What about college? Living in a dorm? Getting married and having children of her own one day? Were these beautiful parts of life out of the question for her? The thoughts collided in his mind, and he felt ill.

"I have to take a break from this, Sam."

Samantha watched her husband walk away. He ran a hand through his dark hair as he walked to the staircase, his head down. She turned back to her work. She wanted to have the kitchen finished before Sue left at six.

CHAPTER 4

Samantha wiped her sweaty palms on her jeans before she checked her reflection once more in the bathroom mirror. She didn't like the crow's feet that were taking hold under her eyes, and she frowned, making them worse. She mentally scolded herself for taking note of her appearance at all, but it was easier to focus on something as simple as that instead of seeing her daughter after her mandatory forty-eight-hour hospitalization. She'd just signed the consent forms for Violet's formal admission, and before she and Ian went to Violet's floor for a visit, Samantha excused herself to the ladies' room for a moment alone. When she emerged, Ian was waiting in the hallway outside, and he took Samantha's hand. Although they weren't the perfect couple, today he just needed to feel her skin against his—to know that they were on the same team. They walked to the elevators, following the signs to Violet's floor. The ride up was silent. Both Samantha and Ian were lost in their own fears.

They exited the elevator when they reached the appropriate floor, and Samantha led the way to the room number the administrator gave them. When she walked into the stark room, she put on her sunniest smile. Violet was lying in an adjustable bed, watching the small television bolted to the wall.

"Hey, baby," Samantha said, perhaps too happily. She was thrilled to see her daughter, but she immediately questioned whether she'd put too much sunshine in her voice. To Samantha's relief, Violet returned her smile.

"Hey!" Violet sat up. She was genuinely happy to see her parents and sat up to give them both hugs.

"I'm feeling much better now," Violet said after she'd embraced both of her parents. "Dr. Geller says I have to stay for a little while, though."

Samantha nodded, fighting back tears at Violet's earnest assessment.

"Yes, angel," Ian said, taking Violet's hand and sitting next to her on the bed. "You're going to be here for a little while. But we're going to come visit you every day."

"That's okay. Everyone is nice," Violet said.

"I'm so glad to hear that. You've got to get better now," Samantha said, taking her daughter's other hand and standing by the bed.

"I wasn't taking my medicine. That was a bad choice." Violet cast her green eyes downward. She wanted to be a good girl, and even though she knew the difference between right and wrong, sometimes she seemed to watch herself do awful things, like she had no choice. Now, she needed to say that she'd done wrong and would try to do better, and everything would be okay again.

"Do you promise that you'll take your medicine from now on, Vi?" Samantha pursed her lips, silencing herself. She didn't want to shame her daughter, but she knew that Violet still hadn't realized the consequences of her actions. She'd gone off her medications, her explosive behaviors had nearly scared her parents to death, and now all Samantha got was a half-baked confession?

"I promise, Mom." As quickly as Violet showed her remorse, Samantha saw the switch flip in her eyes as she turned to her father. "Dad, a car show is on. I know how much you like them. Do you want to watch it with me?" Violet turned to her father with the smile he couldn't say no to.

"I'd love to." Ian pulled a chair around so that he could keep his position at Violet's side. "My two favorite girls and cool cars—I'll be in heaven!"

Samantha watched her husband and daughter watching the small television and tried to contain the seething anger she felt course through her veins. While she was relieved that her daughter was doing well and that the hospital was working to get her regulated again on her medication, she was devastated that despite this close call, Violet could not be humbled. She continued to manipulate her parents, trying to appease them with her charm. Samantha didn't know what to do with the rage. It wasn't fair to be angry at Violet; her daughter couldn't help it. But Samantha had reached a place where she could no longer contain the bitterness that tainted each benign action her daughter made.

• • •

"Violet is such a sweetheart." Sheila Miren knew how to start a meeting with parents. She tapped her short fingernails against the conference table; parents weren't the only ones who were a little nervous about these meetings. "I've been able to spend some time with her, and she's just stolen my heart." She smiled broadly at Samantha and Ian, who smiled back at her, disarmed.

"She can be really wonderful. I just hate that you had to meet her under these circumstances," Samantha said, relieved that she didn't feel under attack. Her anger had subsided while watching her daughter's doughy hand grasping her father's, and besides, her anger with her daughter was *hers*. She'd defend Violet to the death to anyone else who tried to intervene.

"As am I, for all of us. The reason that I wanted to meet with you today isn't to discuss Violet's background or to get any more information about the past. We have two weeks with her here, but I want to already shift our focus to the future—to Violet's transition back home, if you're planning on having her at home."

"Of course we're going to have her back at home," Ian said defensively. "She's our daughter."

"Yes, she is," Sheila said, leaning forward, "and I wasn't making any implications. That's what this meeting is for—to discuss your options and determine a course of action."

Samantha put a hand on Ian's knee as he bristled. She, too, was caught off guard by the implication that they might not take her home. Where else would Violet go? Who else would put up with her manipulation and her lies? Who else would appreciate the freckles on her nose beneath her glasses? The sweet giggle that she emitted when listening to pop music?

"Violet 'graduated' from high school last month," Samantha said, using air quotes on the word *graduated*. "The school was kind enough to allow her to walk with her class. Anyway, we planned on having a neighbor's daughter sit with her during the day. The girl used to babysit Violet, so she's familiar enough with Prader-Willi that we felt we could trust her. But with the events of the past few weeks . . ." Samantha looked again at Ian, who staunchly avoided her gaze. "I don't think that's reasonable."

"My parents will keep her during the day while we work. I own a private practice," he explained to Sheila. "I really only have to work four days a week, if they're long days."

Samantha drew back in surprise. "But your parents are all the way out in Clinton. What about the commute?"

"I'll take her on the train in the morning," Ian countered. "It's only a forty-five minute ride on the train."

"One way. In taking her, coming back to work, retrieving her, and bringing her back, that's three hours on the train every day, Ian."

"There's wifi. It will be fine." Ian turned to Sheila. "My parents live on a small farm. Violet loves the animals there, and my parents are getting older and could use the help. Their house is already equipped to care for Violet's specific needs, and I think it would be a great option."

Samantha looked at Ian right in the eye. "It's not the worst idea in the world, but I don't know how it would work. And," she added, more quietly, "I wish you'd discussed this with me first." She offered Sheila an apologetic smile.

"Samantha, they're our only option right now. Mom offered when Violet got out of school. I just never said anything to you about it because I knew you were so dead set on your own plan. I had a contingency, and with the events of the past few days, I haven't had the time to tell you about it." Ian's voice was curt, and Samantha knew that he didn't draw that line often, but when he did, he meant it.

"Okay. We'll give it a shot." Samantha agreed, raising her eyebrows and looking at Sheila.

Sheila nodded. "That sounds like a reasonable short-term solution. But," she added carefully, "you should know that you do have other options. If you're ever interested in exploring those, just let me know. I'll be more than happy to help you with that."

"Thank you," Samantha said, smiling at her, though the words *other options* rang forebodingly in her mind.

...

"Now, you remember to help Grammy and Pop. You use your best manners, and you take great care of them. You're such a good girl, Violet. They're so excited to be with you," Ian looked into his daughter's green eyes. He had taken the early morning train to Rockville with her. This was their first trip to her grandparents' house since Violet's release from the hospital.

"Yes, Daddy." Violet smiled at him. "I will help Grammy clean up the house, and then Pop will let me drive the tractor with him."

Violet was excited to spend time with her grandparents. She'd always been close to them.

"Pop is waiting in the station to get you. He'll be right past the ticketing agent. You're to go right to him. Do you understand?" Ian asked. His nerves would be on fire until his father called his cell phone to let him know that they were back at home. "Should I get off and walk with you? Will you be okay?"

"I'm eighteen years old, Daddy. I can walk to Pop from the train," Violet was anxious to get off the train. She'd been watched for two weeks and was ready to get a moment without eyes on her.

"Okay. Stick out your tongue." Ian leaned in to examine Violet's mouth.

"I already did!" Violet tapped her toes to the ground in frustration, but she obliged her father and stuck out her tongue. The train came to a stop, and the doors opened. "Geez, Dad," she added. "Forty-five minutes would be a long time to hide medicine in my mouth."

Ian couldn't help laughing at that. It had been an hour since Samantha had given Violet her pills at breakfast. "Be good, Vi," he said, though his daughter was already halfway down aisle. "I love you!" he called. He took a deep breath as Violet tried to scurry her large frame into the train station. Though he'd never "give away" his daughter the way so many fathers did on her wedding day, he now had an idea of what that felt like.

. . .

"Pop!" Violet exclaimed and embraced her grandfather. He smelled like peppermint and aftershave, and when his scent hit her nose, she felt like she'd truly come home again.

"Hey, Purple." Pop returned her hug, using his nickname for his only granddaughter. "Ready to go?"

Violet nodded and followed him into the parking lot to his green Ford pickup that he'd driven longer than she'd been alive. "What's Grammy doing?"

"Getting everything ready for you," Pops said, smiling. "I think she may have some crafts up her sleeve today."

"Are we going to knit?" Violet asked, almost frantically.

"You'll have to wait and see." Pop gave her a wink before turning on the radio and pulling onto a small county road that led to his house.

Violet had always lived in the city, and every time she came to Grammy and Pop's house, she was reminded that the world was bigger than she'd ever imagined. Trees and flowers scattered without symmetry here, the grass would grow higher than her waist if no one cut it, and the world wasn't covered in steam rising off concrete in the summer or black sludge that had originally floated white and puffy from the sky. Violet rolled down her window and breathed in, deep. She felt like she could catch the breeze coming down the side of Pop's pickup and fly away if she wanted.

When Violet entered her grandparents' home, she wasn't struck by the variety of yarn Grammy had laid out across the kitchen table or the watercolors that were stacked on the kitchen counter; but by the smell of the biscuits that lingered from Grammy's morning baking. The air was thick with buttermilk and flour, and Violet's mouth watered in anticipation.

"My sweet girl!" Grammy rushed over to the front door when she heard Pop's key. She kissed her granddaughter on both cheeks.

"Grammy, Daddy wanted me to tell you that he didn't have time to feed me breakfast this morning," Violet said as she returned her grandmother's embrace. "He wanted to know if I could have breakfast here." She pushed out her lips enough to emulate a pout, and her eyes looked desperately ravenous.

"Violet. Your daddy told me that he fed you breakfast before you got on the train. He called to let me know that you were on your way with Pop. Now, listen here, you're not going to tell me stories, are you? I won't put up with it." Grammy cut her eyes at Violet, just enough to let her know that she was serious.

A few hours later, Pop was out on the tractor alone and Grammy had dozed off in front of the soap opera she insisted on watching. Violet got up from her spot on the couch and crept past Grammy's chair, watching her chest rise and fall with her rhythmic snoring. Once Violet got into the hallway, she wasn't sure what to do. The kitchen was locked, and she knew what kind of trouble she could get into there, so she tried to avoid it. She ran her fingers along the frames of the family photos that were carefully hung. Grammy's hallway displayed generations of people, most of whom Violet didn't know, but she loved the family picture that Grammy had in a place of honor. Violet was about six when it was taken, and she remembered fighting with her brother Mitchell all that day. Somehow, when the photographer snapped his shutter, Violet's whole family was smiling at the same time. Six-year-old Violet was missing her front teeth, and she remembered how everyone in first grade called her snaggletooth. It was better than the names that her classmates came up with later, but it was her initiation into being different than everyone else. Moving past the picture, she peeked into Grammy and Pop's bedroom. Grammy's dressing table was perfectly set with the lotions and make-up that she used each day, and Violet just couldn't resist trying on some of the ointments used by the fairer sex.

She looked at herself in the mirror and pushed her brown hair behind her ears. She'd always hated her freckles and found a powder that could cover them up. When she pulled the powder puff from its box, she was struck. She'd found Grammy's hiding place for money.

Violet looked behind her to make sure that no one would come in. She carefully pulled the bills out and unrolled them. Grammy had close to one hundred dollars in ones and fives. If Violet had money, she could do whatever she wanted. She could buy food that no one would know about. She knew that stealing was bad, but she didn't think Grammy would notice if she took just a few dollars. Folding them, she put them in her pocket and put everything back where she'd found it. Just when she was sure she'd gotten away with it, she heard Grammy's voice behind her.

"Got into my makeup, did you?"

Violet jumped and turned around, terrified that she'd been caught stealing.

"Don't be scared. I'm not mad. You're a young lady and . . ." Grammy trailed off. "What if I made up your face? We'll wash it off before you go home, but wouldn't it be fun to play beautician?" Grammy moved closer to Violet, pulling up another chair.

"I would like that very much!" Violet leaned in and closed her eyes, excited to see what she looked like with a new face.

. . .

"Since you've been doing so well at Grammy and Pop's, we have a surprise for you." Samantha sat down next to her daughter on her bed. Violet had been staying with her grandparents for six weeks, and Samantha was surprised at how well the arrangement had been working out, despite her initial skepticism.

"Really? What kind of surprise?" Violet's eyes lit up. She loved surprises.

"I have to work a little late tomorrow, so what if you tried riding the train home by yourself?" Samantha's face conveyed her excitement at the new arrangement. "This is a real privilege, but if it works out, maybe we can start doing it more. You are to get out of Pop's truck, get directly on the six o'clock train, and be here by seven. I'll be waiting for you at the station."

Violet squealed. "Yes! I want to ride the train by myself! That would be so wonderful!"

"You're a grown lady with a cell phone. We trust you to handle this. Are you sure that you can?" Samantha asked.

"Yes! I am grown. I can do it! I promise!" Violet hugged her mother.

"You know to call if anything goes wrong or different, right? We would be worried otherwise," Samantha warned.

"Yes! Mom, I can do it, I promise," Violet giggled.

. . .

Samantha looked at her watch—seven-thirty. The six o'clock train from Rockville had already arrived, but Violet had not been among the passengers who had disembarked. Samantha called Violet's cell phone as she paced back and forth through the station. It rang three times and went to voicemail. Breathing deeply to stay calm, Samantha took a seat on a bench and dialed her mother-in-law.

"Thanks for letting us know she's home!" Samantha's mother-in-law answered brightly.

"That's the thing, Cindy," Samantha said, her stomach dropping with her mother-in-law's greeting. "She isn't. Did Harold take her to the train station?"

Cindy was silent for a moment. When she spoke, her voice trembled. "He did. He stood in the station until the train departed, just to make sure she got on safely. Where do you think she is?"

"Did Harold *see* her get on the train?" Samantha was panicked now. She remembered Dr. Kraemer asking her the same question about Violet's medication a few months ago. Even as she asked, the question sounded silly; it *would* be silly if you were operating with a typical eighteen-year-old—but Violet was not typical. The thought broke Samantha's heart.

"Well, I—I don't know. I'm sure that he did the very best he could, Sam." Cindy's voice grew an edge of defensiveness that was familiar to Samantha.

"I'm sure he did too, Cindy. Listen, I'll call you when I find her. I'm going to drive out your way." Samantha ended the call, threw her phone inside her purse, and headed to her car.

When she pulled out of the parking garage, she realized that she didn't know what to do. The train was a commuter, so there weren't stops along the way. Violet clearly wasn't in the city, but somewhere in Rockville. Samantha took a deep breath and steadied herself for the drive. Where could she be? Why wasn't she answering her phone? Flashes of every terrifying thing in the world came to Samantha. Men with knives and lascivious demands, dirty needles, drugs, speeding cars. Samantha shook her head. She couldn't go there, not yet. Now was not a time for panic but for resolution. She thought about calling Ian, but she knew that he was working late. This was something she had to handle on her own.

After driving a three-mile perimeter around the train

station, Samantha could no longer fight her panic—and, now, guilt. She'd wasted so much time! What would Ian say when he realized she'd driven around, without a focus, while their daughter was missing, without even *calling* him? Suddenly, all of Samantha's decisions seemed unreasonable. What were they thinking, letting Violet spend the days with her grandparents? What was *Samantha* thinking, allowing her daughter to take the train home alone? She reached for her phone, ready to call the police, when she finally caught a familiar silhouette. Violet was sitting by a window at a Waffle House, fork raised to her lips and a stack of empty plates before her.

Samantha pulled into the parking lot, shifted the car into park, and rushed inside.

"Violet! We were so worried about you!" Samantha ran to her daughter, unsure whether to hug or slap Violet as the relief and agony washed over her.

Violet looked up at her mother as if nothing was amiss. "Hey, Mom. I'm eating dinner."

Samantha sat down across the booth from her. "What have you been doing? What are all these plates?"

"All you can eat waffles!" Violet said brightly. "You can only get two pieces of bacon or sausage and two scrambled eggs, but they keep the waffles coming until you say stop. I haven't said stop."

Just then, the waitress walked over to the table. She was in her sixties with grey roots poking through the bottom of her bleached bouffant. Her name tag read "Sally," and Samantha wondered if that was her real name.

"She can just pack them away, can't she now?" Sally winked at Samantha as she sat the new plate before her daughter. "And what can I get you, hon? The same?"

"No, thank you," Samantha tried to keep her cool. She knew that she couldn't take the waffles away from Violet now that they were already in her possession, which left Samantha unsure where to place her anger. On Violet for breaking the carefully placed rules of their new arrangement? On Sally for serving an enormous amount of food to an obviously overweight teenager? On Ian for trying to make Violet's situation fit neatly into an "easy fix?" Or on herself, for being too selfish to cancel the late meeting? "I'll just have a black coffee," Samantha said to the waitress, forcing a smile.

When Sally left, Samantha tried to be practical with her daughter. "Violet, how were you going to pay for this? You don't have any money."

"I got it, Mom," Violet said between mouthfuls.

"Where did you get money?" Samantha demanded. "You shouldn't have any money, you know that."

"I work with Grammy and Pop. They give me money," Violet retorted coolly.

Samantha was enraged. Her in-laws knew better than to give Violet money. Why would they choose to betray her and Ian? Violet wasn't a typical grandchild who could be indulged against the wishes of the parents; she had specific needs. Samantha wondered if they were also overfeeding her. She made a mental note to have that conversation with them later but wanted to continue with Violet now. "This wasn't our agreement. You can't do this. Do you know how sick with worry I was?"

In an instant, Violet's demeanor changed. "I'm an adult!" she screamed. "I have a job to take care of Grammy and Pop during the day. I take care of everything. It's fine that I wanted to have a little dinner alone!"

"Violet, I—" Samantha tried to remain calm, but her daughter's reaction burned her to the core. Violet's swift mood change indicated that she was cycling and that perhaps she wasn't taking her medication as she'd claimed.

"Screw you, Mom! You call me an adult, but you won't let me go to college. You won't let me even go eat by myself. I'm done with this. I'm done with you. It's not fair! Mitchell hates your guts, too—he told me so. And I get it because I feel the same way!" Violet shoved the remaining quarter of the waffle in her mouth before getting up and running out of the restaurant.

Having no idea what to do, Samantha threw a twenty on the table, hoping it covered the cost of the meal, and ran out after her. Violet was not in the parking lot, and Samantha knew how sneaky her daughter could be despite her lumbering frame. Samantha would have a better chance of finding her in the car than on foot. She buckled her seatbelt and took off, shining her headlights into alleys and searching for her daughter. After forty-five minutes, with nothing turning up, Samantha tearfully called Ian.

"She disappeared. I found her in a Waffle House in Rockville. She yelled at me and walked out. I can't find her. It's been almost an hour."

"Whoa. Sam, what are you talking about?"

"Violet didn't get off the train at seven. I went looking for her. I found her, but now she's gone. I don't know what to do. She said she agreed with Mitch—that I'm a terrible mother." Samantha's tears finally flowed.

"I'm going to call the police. Go to that Waffle House in case she goes back. I'm on my way down there, too." Ian hung up, and Samantha found herself stung that he didn't offer her any reassurances or even a simple "I love you" before he cut the line, leaving her alone in the small town fifty miles away from him.

CHAPTER 5

Violet had been enrolled in public school since kindergarten. It had been a long road for her and her parents. Her IEP, or Individualized Education Plan, hadn't changed much since kindergarten. She was classified OHI, or Other Health Impaired, since she suffered with a genetic syndrome that affected her both physically and mentally. She still attended speech and occupational therapy through her school, but her communication skills had greatly improved, as had her ability to grip small pencils for writing in print. She could confidently speak in entire sentences by sixth grade, and although she couldn't follow more than one direction at a time still, she did each step with such purpose that her teachers were always impressed with her compliance. Her specialized services were primarily to meet her physical needs, such as having an escort through the hallways and during her lunch period. When Violet did act out in her classes, she quickly recovered and usually apologized with a hug. Most students knew exactly who she was, and while some could be mean, most couldn't help but have a soft spot for the friendly, talkative girl.

Violet's junior year of high school was the first year that she wouldn't have Mitchell with her, as he'd graduated and gone away to college. The transition was rough on her, because Mitchell had been the one who'd walked Violet to all of her classes during the passing period and had lunch with her to guard her from the food issues. He'd received credit for community service hours from the school in exchange for sacrificing most of his social life his junior and senior years. The amount of hours that he'd gained by graduation, in addition to the heart-wrenching essay that he'd written about life with his sister, had gained him acceptance to his first-choice school, despite his low GPA and lack of involvement with any extracurricular activities.

Although Mitchell was gone, Violet's IEP still indicated that she needed supervision constantly, especially during passing periods and lunch. Violet's paraprofessional, who was with her in each class, would walk the passing period with her, leaving lunch as a critical vacancy. The school arranged for Violet to have a "buddy" during those times—another student at the school. Ian and Samantha were skeptical of the arrangement: they could trust Mitchell to understand exactly what Violet needed, but they weren't sure that another student would grasp the gravity of the situation. However, their hands were tied, so they agreed to the arrangement.

Violet's buddy was a senior classmate, Jessica, who had a good rapport with Violet and needed the community service hours for a scholarship she was pursuing.

The second week into the school year, Jessica was distracted for just a few seconds by another student. When she turned back to Violet, she only found an empty seat at the table next to her. She looked around, frantic that Violet had escaped the alcove where they ate their lunch.

Jessica rushed into the main cafeteria just in time to see Violet swipe four cookies from the tray of one of her classmates. The student, a freshman who didn't know Violet, didn't immediately recognize that she had special needs. Trying to show off how tough he was, he stood up to her.

"Hey! Fatass! What do you think you're doing? You can't just take things that don't belong to you!" He stood at least six inches taller than Violet, staring down into her face.

Violet shoved a cookie into her mouth in response. She didn't care who he was or that the cookies weren't hers or that she wasn't supposed to be in here. No one understood what it was like to be her, with a hunger she didn't just feel but *heard*. It was like a roaring in her ears, the loudness of waterfalls that got even louder when she could *smell* the food, see it all around her, and everyone just expected her to mind her own business, eat her own stupid little sandwich that did nothing to quiet the roar in her belly? It wasn't fair! She gobbled the second cookie, glaring up at the boy who was yelling at her.

"What the hell? I don't care that you're a girl, or a retard, you're being disrespectful, and I don't handle disrespect." The student picked up his water bottle from the table and twisted off the cap. In a motion too quick for anyone, including Jessica, to stop, he squeezed the bottle over Violet's head, drenching her finely braided hair and soaking the remaining cookies in her hand. Violet screamed, wiping her face, and Jessica saw the primal anger in her eyes. Unconsciously, the senior helper took two steps back and bumped into another student. A crowd had gathered to watch the unfolding drama.

Violet was in a red, mean world. She went there some-times, when people made her mad, and she thought she could do anything when she was there. Now she looked at the student who had humiliated her, and she hated him. Hated his stupid messy hair and his skinny arms and his black shirt and especially hated that he was *normal!* He didn't need those cookies, and she did. She shoved him with two open hands, and he tripped back-wards over his seat, clocking his head on the ground. Violet stood over him, screaming profanities, and in be-tween, she reached for the pizza that was still on his tray and shoved as much of it in her mouth as she could. The delicious, greasy cheesiness filled her with such a surge of pleasure that she forgot about the boy.

Mrs. Posey, the assistant principal at the high school, was only two weeks into her job. She didn't know Violet's situation, so she blindly made her way to the action.

"What are you doing?" she exclaimed. "Back up right now, young lady!"

"Fuck you, old lady," Violet roared, swatting the woman away from her and balling the piece of pizza into her mouth, grease falling to her elbows in viscous drops.

The entire cafeteria burst into laughter, then applause. Although Mrs. Posey was new to the school, she'd al-ready cracked down on the student body for things that the previous vice principal had let slide: in the last two weeks, dress code violations, tardiness, and skipping were already seeing a referral and punishment rate that surpassed the entirety of the previous school year.

"I will not stand for this," Mrs. Posey announced. "From any of you. Young lady, you are to follow me to my office right now."

Violet ignored her. She grabbed the boy's tater tots from his tray and shoved them into her mouth.

"What a fat retard," the boy said from the ground, and without thinking, Violet kicked him right in the ribs. She'd never been very coordinated, so her shoe only made grazing contact, but he still yelped. Then, as quickly as it had come on, the red world started to lose its color.

"The way you're conducting yourself is unacceptable," Mrs. Posey said. "You have to come with me."

Violet was still shaking with anger, but she turned to Mrs. Posey, prepared to follow her to her office.

Mrs. Posey deposited Violet in the waiting area and called Samantha at work.

"I'm sure you can understand that I cannot take this kind of behavior lightly, Mrs. Durkin," Mrs. Posey said, after she'd recounted the story. "I'm afraid that my only option is expulsion. She can attend the Wilcox School for troubled students, and that's a generous offer."

Samantha was taken aback by the vice principal's manner. She took a deep breath, choosing her words wisely as she composed her counter-argument. "Mrs. Posey, you'll see from Violet's paperwork that she has Prader-Willi Syndrome, which has a variety of rare and unique symptoms. We had our reservations about Jessica accompanying Violet to the cafeteria, but we thought we'd give it a shot. Violet seeks food. Her brain is wired to a drive state, where she constantly feels as if she is suffering from starvation. If you were actually, *literally*, starving to death, would you be afraid to drop an f-bomb on anyone who tried to come between you and a meal?"

"Well, no. But, that . . . that attitude will not be tolerated. I can't have that happening here." Mrs. Posey was thrown off by Samantha's analogy but had to stand her ground in this situation.

"Mrs. Posey, if you'll work with me, and with Violet's psychiatrist and teachers, you'll find that she is the sweetest girl. She can be compliant, and with an IQ of 69, she can keep up with the material presented in her special education classes. I promise that pulling Violet out of school and into an alternative program will not prove helpful to her. We will make this work." Samantha's tone was desperate. She knew that Mrs. Posey could reach her daughter, if only she'd give her a chance.

"I'd like to have a meeting regarding her IEP one more time," Mrs. Posey said. "We'll have all the necessary players there, and hopefully we can work out something that will work for everyone. I'm going to give Violet one more chance, because I believe that all teenagers, regardless of their circumstances, deserve that. But if I have one more outburst of this kind from her, regardless of her condition, she's done."

Mrs. Posey's voice was professional, but Samantha could sense that she had a heart. "We may not be able to keep her from outbursts completely," she said honestly, "but if we can all work together, you'll find a drastic reduction—and nothing like what happened today."

"Let's certainly hope not."

CHAPTER 6

Ian had just gotten Violet settled in her bed and gone to the couch when his cell phone rang. The caller ID told him it was his mother, and he answered, utterly exhausted.

"Is she home? Is everything okay?" Ian's mother's voice was tearful.

"She's fine. I just got her in bed. Samantha's a wreck. She's in bed too," Ian said wearily. "Thank you for offering to help earlier. I really appreciate it."

"Violet's my little girl, too. Keep in mind I only ever had boys until she came along." Ian could hear that relief in his mother's voice. "Ian, tonight may not be the time to have this conversation, but . . ." she trailed off. Ian knew that whatever she was going to say pained her, and he wasn't looking forward to more bad news.

"What is it, Mom?"

"Well, I was in my room getting ready to come and help you search for Violet. I keep a little cash in my vanity—not much, just a little spending money. Well, I went in there to grab the money in case we needed it for anything, and it's gone. I don't want to make any accusations, but Violet plays with my make-up from time to time, and she's the only one who's had access to it. I think she took it, Ian. After that, and tonight, I don't know how much help we can be." Her voice broke with emotion.

Ian rubbed the bridge of his nose with his thumb and forefinger. Violet had stolen from his parents? He felt both violated and guilty of violation; that his own child would steal from his eighty-year-old mother. "Mom, I'm so sorry. How much was it? I'll replace it."

"No need to replace it. It was just the cash that I pulled from Dad's pockets on laundry day, but . . ." The sound of his mother's tears shook Ian to the core. He couldn't have his mother crying over *his* hopeless situation.

"Mom, I was going to call you tomorrow anyway and tell you that we need to regroup. If you could just be with her the rest of this week, Samantha and I will find something else by next week, I promise. I already have Friday cleared to be home, so it would only be tomorrow and Thursday. We're in a bit of a lurch here," Ian added, almost to himself. The next three days, he thought, would buy some time to figure out what to do next.

"What if I just come to your house in the morning and stay until Friday night?" his mother suggested. "Then you'll be close if I need you, and you'll have an extra day to create a plan for next week."

"That's perfect, Mom. I appreciate it." Now his own voice echoed the emotion in his mother's. "Thank you. I love you."

They hung up, with Ian agreeing to pick her up from the train station at seven-thirty the next morning. Ian glanced at the clock; it was after midnight.

What are we going to do? he thought, sinking back into the couch. He should be nearing retirement. He and Samantha should be enjoying their lives, out with friends, taking long vacations. They'd *raised* their children. The hard part of life was supposed to be over. But Ian felt like he was drowning in all the might-have-been situations running through his head.

He got up and went to the liquor cabinet. Unlocking it with the key that he kept hidden on the top, he pulled out a highball and a bottle of scotch that he hadn't touched in years. If any time a drink was warranted, it was now. He took his drink out to the patio and had a seat at the table, the thick, fibrous cushions of the chair sinking beneath his weight. For a moment, he pretended that this was normal—that he had a drink on his porch at night when he wanted, that his life wasn't consumed with unimaginable tasks and details that no one ever envisions. The scotch warmed his throat, and he could feel his shoulders relaxing.

Several peaceful minutes passed before the sliding glass door opened behind him. "I couldn't find you," Samantha said sleepily.

"Is everything okay?" Ian asked, instantly on high alert. But Samantha simply took the seat next to him and pulled her knees up to her chest.

"Everything's fine. I woke up and the house was quiet. I looked in on Violet. She is sleeping peacefully."

Ian sat the glass of scotch between them on the white metal table. Samantha picked it up and took a drink.

"I forgot how much I like that," she said, a sad smile forming on her face.

"Mom called. She's coming tomorrow morning and is going to stay with us until Friday evening." Ian looked down at the glass that Samantha set between them.

"That's very kind of her," Samantha said carefully. "But I feel like there is a caveat."

Ian looked up. "There is. They can't keep Violet anymore. She's just too much for them."

Samantha looked at Ian, puzzled. "Tonight was terrible, but really? They're going to leave us when we need them the most? Good. It wasn't working out anyway. Did you know that they were giving Violet money? Without that, I doubt she would have ever tried to make a run for it. I should have known better than to trust your parents with anything, especially something as important as the care of their granddaughter. I—"

"Violet stole from them, Sam," Ian said, cutting off his wife's rant. "Mom kept money in her vanity, and it's missing. Violet was the only one who had access. That explains why she was in such a hurry to get to the Waffle House. Also, why she had all the candy wrappers and chip bags on her when I found her earlier."

Samantha was immediately mortified at her outburst. "Oh, God. I'm so sorry, Ian. Violet lied to me." She shook her head, angry with herself for believing her daughter, angry at the world for the fact that she *couldn't* believe her daughter. She took another sip of scotch. "What are we going to do? We can't afford to retire or hire a live-in nurse. Where is Violet going to go?"

Ian cleared his throat. "When we met with Sheila, she mentioned that we have other options when it comes to Violet's care. Remember?"

Samantha looked at her husband. "Other options. Yes, but . . . Ian. What do you think she meant?"

"I don't know, but it's worth investigating."

Samantha reached over and squeezed Ian's hand. As always with Violet, the prospect of a form of help they hadn't explored brought with it wary hope.

CHAPTER 7

Almost two years after Mrs. Posey almost expelled Violet, Samantha's torso fit perfectly into the hard-backed seat of the auditorium. While most people found those seats uncomfortable and almost abusive, Samantha loved that her head was high and her shoulder blades were touching. She had reason to be proud today—although Violet wasn't technically graduating from high school, the school had arranged for Violet to participate in the graduation ceremony. She would be the head usher, marking time for the walking graduates, and she would receive special recognition and a plaque for "Most Improved Senior." Although Violet would be returning to her high school in the fall, Samantha and Ian decided to celebrate their daughter with their friends and family the same way that they celebrated their sons when they graduated.

Samantha looked down the row at the three men in her life. She was thrilled that Lukas had come home from Connecticut to celebrate with Violet. He had just finished his junior year of college and brought a bottle of champagne home to celebrate his news of a doctoral fellowship at Stanford. Mitchell, on the other hand, had stopped attending his freshman classes after spring break. When Ian received Mitchell's grades via email, they were three F's and an Incomplete. He called his son to see what was going on, and Mitchell explained that he needed a year to "find himself," to which Ian responded that Mitchell would be well-served to either move back home or get a job, because he couldn't rely on his parents for financial support if he wasn't attending school. Still raw from the blow Mitchell felt he'd been unfairly served, he sulked into Violet's ceremony like a petulant child. Samantha, ever the optimistic PR professional, had hoped that Mitchell would pull himself out of his funk, if only for a moment to celebrate his sister's and brother's achievements. Of course, she was wrong. He was sitting in the aisle seat, arms crossed and eyes only half open.

Samantha shook off her younger son's mood and leaned over to Ian. "I never thought we'd get here. I'm so proud of Violet, I can't stand it."

"I know," Ian said, his eyes shining. "This is truly a moment for us to celebrate. We've all worked so hard to make this happen—you especially, Sam."

Samantha beamed as the commencement music began, and Violet led the charge of her class, strolling proudly as she caught her mother's eye. The family waved and smiled, and Violet smiled back, but took her role as the usher so seriously that she raised her head regally and continued on her somber task.

Samantha barely heard the customary commencement speeches. She spent the hour leading up to the handing of diplomas staring at her girl. When the vice principal finally stood to read the graduates' names, Samantha was rapt; wondering when her daughter's certificate would come in the ceremony. Samantha waited for the moment when her baby would walk, accept her prize, as anxiously as she'd awaited Violet's entrance into the world. She had been afraid that Violet wouldn't be able to handle the attention, but Violet seemed to be soaking it up, wearing a beaming smile.

"Before we begin with the commencement of graduates, we have a special student here tonight. Violet Julianne Durkin," Mrs. Posey called, and the entire audience stood and cheered. Violet looked out at everyone for a moment, a look of happy surprise on her face. She stood with Mrs. Posey, accepting her plaque and smiling for a picture; then Mrs. Posey wrapped her arms around Violet, and the auditorium roared with the louder cheers and whistles of the audience.

"Two things in one day I never thought I'd see," Samantha said in full volume so that Ian could hear her over the crowd.

Ian nodded his head. "I know!" He had tears in his eyes, and Samantha couldn't tell if they were bittersweet or pure joy.

Although Samantha wasn't a crier, she could relate to his emotional release. Seeing Mrs. Posey embrace their daughter for what seemed like a full minute made Samantha's heart explode. Violet had turned a potential enemy into a big advocate. That was Violet's biggest gift, changing minds, opening understanding. Samantha looked over at her sons. Lukas was alternating between smiling widely and whistling, and Mitchell stood, clapping blandly. She'd brought these three lives into the world, and they were capable of so much—she only wished that she could make her middle son see his own significance, that he would change his mind and open his heart to the world. For now, though, she shifted her attention back to her daughter. It was Violet's time.

Back home, the Durkins had arranged a small party in Violet's honor. They hosted a sit-down dinner so that Violet wouldn't have to battle with a buffet all night, hiring a small catering team to make the plates in the kitchen and serve their guests. After dinner, a staff member asked Samantha if she needed anything else, as they were packing the leftover food for the Durkins' refrigerator. Samantha smiled, thanked them for their time, and told them they could leave. She and Ian would take over hosting duties for the rest of the night, refreshing drinks in the kitchen.

An hour later, Samantha walked into the kitchen balancing three wines glasses in need of refill. She gasped, nearly dropping the glasses: Violet was standing in the light of the open refrigerator, stuffing her mouth full with fried mushrooms and chocolate cake. Next to her stood Mitchell, kitchen keys in hand.

"What the hell is going on in here?" Samantha cried out. "Mitchell!"

Samantha couldn't believe it. After taking responsibility for Violet all through high school, he *knew* how wrong his actions were, yet his eyes were not apologetic but defiant.

"It's her night," he said. "She told me she wanted a snack, and since you and Dad are so busy getting drunk with your cronies, I thought I'd actually serve the guest of honor."

Samantha set the wine glasses on her granite countertop with enough force to fracture two of their stems. "You're not serving anyone! Are you that angry, Mitch? Do you want to kill your sister? Are you that attention-starved?" Samantha's voice shook with anger, with shock at her son's betrayal of his sister.

"I'm only good to you when I can police my sister," Mitchell said. "I spent my whole life as the afterthought behind Lukas's brain and Violet's Prader-Willi—and now it's ironic: I'm the only one who's actually focused on what *she* wants on *her* night of glory. It's fucked up, really." Mitchell closed the door to the refrigerator, locked it, and tossed the keys at his mother. "Vi, enough. You can have something else to eat later."

Violet howled when Mitchell shut the refrigerator door. "Mitch! Open it!" she cried to her brother, who ignored her and walked toward his mother.

Samantha caught the keys on reflex, her eyes never leaving her son's. "Mitchell, the only thing that's screwed up about this is you. Lukas is going to get his Ph.D., Violet overcomes obstacles that you can't even imagine *every single day*, but you—you're the only one who wants to live off us, and why? Because you feel that we *owe* you something?" Samantha heard her voice rising. She knew she was going too far, but she couldn't stop. "You had the same childhood and the same parents as your siblings, but you're immature. You'd put other people in danger just to make a point. I think it's best that you leave now."

"That's exactly what you want, isn't it Mom?" Mitchell's anger saturated his voice to a point where Samantha wasn't sure she recognized it. "You want me to go away so you can focus on your perfect oldest son and your handicapped daughter who you spend all of your time fighting for. You base your worth on how people perceive you as a mother to those two—the two who make you proud or make people feel sorry for you. You're a fraud! You want to forget about your middle child—the one who doesn't have a perfect degree or a syndrome for you to hide behind. Fine. I'm done anyway." Mitchell got his car keys from the kitchen counter behind Violet, whose face was mottled red with frustration and dismay, and stomped out the door leading to the garage.

Samantha was so stunned by the accusing words of her son that she didn't even register that Violet was still screaming until Ian came into the kitchen, "Sam, what is going on?" he said. "I can't keep covering for the muffled shouts everyone's hearing out in the living room."

"I'm a terrible mother. That's all. Please tell our guests that Violet is ill and she and I both have to go to bed. Send my apologies to everyone." Samantha, shell-shocked, led Violet up the stairs to her bedroom.

CHAPTER 8

"I'm sorry for the circumstances that brought you here today, but I'm glad to see you again," Sheila said, taking a seat behind her desk in her small office. Behind her hung pictures that her clients had drawn for her and framed photographs of her with another woman. In one, they sat together on a Harley. In another, they both wore green dresses and hats like they were at a Kentucky Derby themed party, and a third photo showed the two with a pair of brindle pit bull puppies. The women couldn't have been more physically different—Sheila was petite with blonde hair cropped short to her head, and the other woman was mixed-race, with coffee colored skin and large curls of hair protruded from beneath her hat. *Clearly that isn't her sister,* Samantha thought. *What a lovely young couple.*

"Thank you for meeting with us," Ian said, his voice indicating his exhaustion. "I'm keeping my phone on during our meeting, as my mother is at our house with Violet . . ." He trailed off.

"Of course. I understand if you have to cut out," Sheila said, smiling. "Samantha filled me in a little on the phone, but I'd like for you to tell me what the past six weeks have been like in more detail."

The mention of Samantha's name drew her from her musings of the photographs on Sheila's shelf. Wondering about Sheila's personal life was an escape from facing the reason they were in her office. "We've exhausted our personal options," Samantha said, and as soon as the words came out of her mouth, she burst into tears. Her eyes and chest were raw from crying so much, but her body's painful reaction couldn't stop her.

Ian put his arm around his wife and filled Sheila in on the manipulation, the sneaking away, and the stealing that their daughter had partaken in the past few months.

"There are times she seems like an angel, but her behaviors haven't improved in the least since her release from the hospital," Samantha said. "We're doing everything that we can, but we've come to the conclusion that it's time to investigate the other options that you mentioned during our first meeting. School is starting soon, and we can't just send her back as if nothing has changed over the past three months."

"Okay." Sheila paused, as if collecting her thoughts. "Before we begin this discussion, I want to tell you that this is not a reflection of your parenting. There is no shame in wanting the very best for Violet."

Samantha found comfort in Sheila's words, but not enough to squelch the guilt that had taken root at her core. She remembered how she felt when Lukas, her oldest, was a baby. Placing him in the care of a nanny in order to return to work almost killed her, even though she'd made those arrangements while she was still pregnant. The night before she went to work, she nursed her baby and looked into his drowsy eyes. He was such a helpless little creature, and she wasn't sure that her arms would work if they weren't weighed down with his little body. She felt the same way now, even though Violet was, by all accounts, an adult.

Sheila rustled through her desk drawers and came out with a folder of paperwork. "What you've tried with Violet's grandparents is essentially respite care—which is a step that the state would want you to take before exploring other options. Has anyone spoken to you about residential placement before?"

Samantha took a deep breath. On some level, she knew that this was why they'd come to speak to Sheila, but actually hearing the term *residential placement* broke the emotional dam that she'd built up. "The geneticist mentioned it," she whispered, wiping at her damp eyes and looking at Ian. "Remember? When he gave us the diagnosis."

Ian nodded, looking ill.

"So, how would it work?" Samantha asked quietly. "Violet would go live somewhere else—permanently?"

"Nothing is ever permanent," Sheila replied reassuringly. "What we're looking for is a place where Violet can get all the attention, all the specialized care, that she requires. Ideally, we could find a placement for her where she is learning and growing, just as you are."

Those words made Samantha feel better, but she still felt rubbed raw at the prospect of sending Violet away. She looked over at Ian, who put his hand on her knee.

"We're out of options, Sam. We should have explored this months ago, for Violet's sake." Ian turned to Sheila, "How would we move forward investigating this?"

"I can be your advocate through the state," Sheila said, "unless you want to hire someone else. I think that's the first decision that the two of you will want to make."

Ian looked at Samantha, and they both nodded. "We'd like to streamline this process as much as possible," Ian said. "But why do we need an advocate with the state?"

"Residential care is costly, and most parents seek funding for their child through the state, regardless of their financial situation," Sheila responded. "We'll have to get your case approved for funding before we can look into placing Violet."

Ian nodded. "Will we get to pick the place that Violet goes? Her needs are very specific, and she can't live anywhere where they don't understand Prader-Willi."

"You'll have a say, certainly, if you can prove to the state that one facility will meet Violet's needs better than another. Homes specifically designed for Prader-Willi are rare. The state funding systems prefer that in-state residential programs be utilized first, however. It is very difficult to get approval for an out-of-state placement, which is considered a last resort." Sheila opened the folder and pulled out a form that listed all of the residential care facilities in the state and placed it before Ian and Samantha.

Ian ignored the paper in front of him. "Well, are there any homes in this state that specialize in Prader-Willi? We'd want to have her as close as possible."

Sheila grimaced but covered it up well. "Homes specifically designed for Prader-Willi are rare," she repeated.

"Rare . . . okay, but that means they do exist, right?" Ian pressed. "Where are they? What do you know about them?"

Sheila looked down at her folder again. "Well, after Samantha called, I did some research. I had never heard of Prader-Willi before meeting Violet, and after reading her psychiatric evaluation and some of her charts from Dr. Kraemer's extensive work with her, I figured that I should be prepared to answer any questions you may have. I have found a program called Prader-Willi Homes of Oconomowoc, or PWHO. It's in Oconomowoc, Wisconsin, and was the first program of its kind. They've been working exclusively with people with Prader-Willi for more than thirty-five years."

Samantha's eyes widened. "Wait, so this facility is *only* for people with Prader-Willi?"

"It is. I compiled all of my research here. Please take your time looking it over." Sheila added the paper to the stack for the Durkins to review.

"We'd need to look into it further," Ian said, "but if it's really the best place for her, how can we get her there—if that's the route that we decide to go?"

"When do you need to have care for Violet?" Sheila asked matter-of-factly.

"Monday, if possible," Samantha replied, thinking that the timeline was so short.

"Here's the deal." Sheila looked around. "We can't get Violet anywhere by Monday going the traditional route. However, with Dr. Kraemer's diagnoses, and her running away from the care that you have reasonably provided for your daughter, I can file a petition for crisis placement. The state will cover her emergency placement while we work to get some long-term funding in place."

"Crisis placement? They'll just throw Violet somewhere to get her out of our hair?" Samantha was livid. "Can't we just get approved and get her where we want her? Is this going to be a complicated mess? Because that's exactly what I don't need any more of in our lives!"

Ian put his hand on Samantha's knee. "Sam, I hate this as much as you do, but what else can we do? Are you going to take another two weeks off work to stay home with Violet? Am I? I've lost a third of my patients this summer due to my scheduling conflicts, and if I continue at this rate, I'll be out of business by August. We can't afford for either of us to lose our jobs or income right now. No one wants to 'throw Violet away,' but we have to find somewhere else for her to live if we want any hope of a bright future for any of us."

Samantha hated that he was right. A part of her still didn't want to believe that she couldn't manage her household. But she needed help. So did Violet. Every time that she acted out, every time she hurt herself, Samantha felt that she was failing her daughter. Violet needed to live somewhere that she was safe. She needed constant attention from people who knew how to take care of her. Besides, Samantha was tired of being Violet's prison guard. She wanted to be her mother again. "Agreed," she said in a small voice. "Do you promise that Violet will be safe and happy where she goes?" she asked Sheila.

"I will do the best that I can," Sheila said. "I promise you that. We'll want her to be close to home so that you can go visit frequently, just like you did in the hospital. Your involvement and input is crucial here. And remember, the facility we place her in might be perfect for Violet; we may not have to move her to Wisconsin when the funding is figured out. I just need the two of you to fill out the paperwork in that packet, and I'll get started on the crisis funding this afternoon. I anticipate that we'll be able to get Violet into a facility by Sunday."

"What facility, though?" Ian cut in. "Who will pick it?"

"Dr. Durkin, I understand that you don't want your child to go anywhere she won't be safe. We share the same concerns, and please know that I will work with the state. We have to go where her needs are best met, but there must be an opening. In the meantime, research the other facilities that I've laid out so that when your funding is approved, we can get her where she needs to be long term."

Samantha picked up the pen and looked over the piles of paperwork before her. Fear and relief simultaneously washed over her. She had no idea what the future held, but she hoped that at least she could get Violet out of any immediate danger.

CHAPTER 9

"Alright, Vi, it's time to take your medicine." Samantha leaned toward her daughter, depositing three pills on the table before her. She tried to keep her demeanor positive, although the past two weeks had been anything but bright. Lukas returned to Connecticut the day after Violet's party. He had a full load of summer classes to attend. The next day, Mitchell finally came home just to pack his things and leave again, without speaking to either of his parents or Violet. Samantha had taken two weeks off work to help Violet transition into being at home for the summer, and she was relieved that the time was almost up and she could return to her job, where she had some control.

"Okay, Mom." Violet looked down at the pills on the table. She put them on her tongue and swallowed them down with a gulp of her skim milk.

"Thank you for being so cooperative!" Samantha sat down next to her daughter, placing her hand on Violet's forearm. "You're making such good choices."

Violet smiled. She loved when her mother reassured her, when she looked at her in the eyes and told her what a good girl she was.

"I'm going to water the flowers," Samantha said, rising.

"Do you want to come with me?"

Violet shook her head. "I think I want to paint, Mom." She chose her words carefully so that her speech didn't betray her secret.

"Okay, honey. I'll be back inside in just a few minutes. If you need me . . ."

"I'll get you." Violet smiled again.

Samantha pulled her gardening gloves from their drawer and walked to the sliding glass door that led to their small backyard. She was thankful for the beautiful June weather and thankful that her daughter's behavior was allowing her to get outside and work in the garden. If Violet could maintain her positive attitude, despite all the upheaval of the past two weeks, Samantha was convinced that her daughter would be fine with the neighborhood girl who was home from college and looking for a summer job. Samantha had worked hard in those two weeks to establish a home routine for Violet, and she smiled to herself, pleased with her success as she padded out to the small bed of roses that she'd planted.

As soon as the sliding glass door was securely shut, Violet slid her finger into her mouth and pulled out the dissolving pills from between her tongue and bottom teeth. She shuddered with the bitter trail of taste they left and went into the bathroom, wrapping them in toilet paper and flushing them down the toilet. Forget the medicine. The drugs that Dr. Kraemer had prescribed for her anxiety disorder made her feel like a zombie, walking around with a weird half-smile but doing nothing to silence the trigger in her mind that drove her to quench the hunger. That's what she needed help with anyway—that's where all her problems came from. She didn't want to take medication unnecessarily and was happy to smile at her mom and get the reassurance that she so desperately desired while keeping herself straight.

That night, Violet lay awake, staring at the red numbers on her bedside clock. When it finally struck eleven, she slipped from her bed and into the kitchen. She knew that her parents would be long asleep by now, and it was the perfect time to see what she could find in the kitchen. Every day, her mother hid the keys to the pantry in a different place, but Violet watched her very carefully after dinner. She heard the familiar jingle as she saw the keys slide into the fake drawer in front of the sink. Violet knew that she'd have to be quiet, but she figured that if her parents were sleeping upstairs, she could slide through and gain access to all of her favorite treats.

Violet carefully pulled open the drawer, knowing that it was tight with suspension and would snap back. With heady excitement, she tossed the keys into her pocket and carefully popped the drawer back in place. She made her way over to the pantry, and when the lock provided the satisfying click, indicating that the key worked, her body trembled with anticipation. She grabbed two bags of pretzels and three bottles of chocolate drink before sliding the pantry door closed, locking it and returning the key to its hiding place. Back in her room, Violet greedily consumed the salty sticks, washing them down with room temperature chocolate drink. She'd finished and was ready to go back downstairs, risking it again, when the hall light switched on.

"I guess it was nothing," Violet heard her father's voice call down the hallway. His footsteps were getting closer, so she shoved the wrappers under her pillow and faked sleep as the light from the hallway cast across her bed-room.

"Vi?" Ian called sleepily.

"Yes, Daddy?" Violet made her voice sound equally tired.

"You doing okay?"

"Yes. I just had to go to the bathroom." Violet's voice dripped with sweetness.

"Okay. Sweet dreams, angel." Ian shut the door to Violet's room and went back to bed.

Each night had been much the same for the past two weeks. Violet knew that her mother wanted to believe she was fine, so she wasn't checking her weight or hiding the keys to the kitchen in a different place. Even without a scale, though, which Violet avoided like the hissing, venomous thing it was, she knew the late-night snacks were taking their toll. She wore baggy shirts over her jeans so that no one could tell they were unbuttoned and half-unzipped, and avoided the cute dresses her mother bought her for walking at graduation, as she just knew they were too tight.

The night before her mother returned to work, Violet got brave. She decided that she could sneak out of the house and walk to the store just as easily as she could break into the kitchen, and as a bonus, no one would notice things disappearing! She could buy whatever she wanted, eat *whatever she wanted*. Her parents hadn't guarded the money she'd received as "graduation" gifts. Most of the cards were packed tight with ten-, twenty-, fifty-, or one-hundred-dollar bills. The sense of possibility engulfed her, occupying all her thoughts. She opened her nightstand drawer and rifled around until she found the sock with the bills tucked inside. She pulled the money out and was delighted to find a twenty. As quietly as she could, avoiding all the creaky floorboards in the old house, she crept to the garage door, disabled the alarm, and walked out the side door.

The walk was longer than Violet imagined. They passed the store so fast in the car! Just a few minutes and there it was, brightly lit, with plastic bags catching the light on the shelves and Violet craning her neck to see if she could make out exactly what type of snacks there were, until Mom noticed and called her attention to something else, as if Violet were so easily distracted. But walking—at night, of all times—was a different story. She could hardly see the sidewalk in front of her and squinted in sudden fear whenever headlights flashed. But she tucked her head down and kept going. With each step, she could feel how heavy she was, and the farther she got from home, the more she dreaded the return walk. But she was on a mission, like a soldier marching onwards, and soon she'd see the beautifully glowing gas station and get her reward.

It took her a solid forty minutes, but finally, Violet made it. She sprinted the last several feet, bursting through the door with such fervor that the clerk was startled from half-sleep in front of a small television. Panting, she smiled at him, and he gave an uncertain smile back as she lunged toward the aisles, grabbing indiscriminately.

The clerk had to give Violet two bags to carry all of her goods from the store, and she felt a surge of relief as she walked outside and shoved a snack cake into her mouth. The dough got sticky when it mixed with her saliva, but she washed it down with one of the twenty-ounce cans of soda that she bought. With a strange mix of adrenaline and exhaustion, Violet sank to the sidewalk to enjoy her feast. When she was done, she collected all of the trash into one of the plastic bags and threw it away in the trashcan that was on the corner. She went back into the store but realized that she didn't have any more money when she was in the chip aisle. She looked around. The clerk was back to watching TV, leaning on the counter lazily. No one else was here. Without further thought, she stuffed a bag of tortilla chips under her shirt. Then she went to the candy bar aisle and slid two candy bars into her bra and stuffed her pockets with several more. She was trying to stick a roll of mints into her sock when the clerk approached her.

"What are you doing?" he asked, eyeing her.

"Nothing!" Violet exclaimed. "Just shopping."

"Listen, I know that you're trying to take things. Just put them back and leave," he said.

"I'm not doing anything!" Violet protested.

The clerk sighed, looking at her more closely. "I don't want to call the cops," he said, "but if you don't put the food back and leave, I'll have no choice."

"I'm not stealing! You're stealing!" Violet screamed, as if a switch flipped inside. She was frantic. How was she going to get out of the store with her food?

"Calm down," the clerk demanded. "That was unnecessary. You're the one in the wrong here."

But Violet wasn't wrong—she was just hungry. She let out a shriek as she tried to shove past the clerk. Her weight knocked him off balance, and he fell against one of the shelves, sending its contents clattering to the floor. For a moment, Violet and the clerk stared at each other. Then he picked up the phone and called the police.

The thing was, this was Violet's chance. She knew the

police wouldn't be there for another few minutes, and the clerk was down, so what was stopping her from grabbing whatever she wanted? Nothing. She went wild, running through the store and pulling whatever she could into her arms.

"Man, what the hell?" the clerk asked. He was staring at her with delighted repulsion. Violet busied herself, dumping bags and boxes down the collar of her shirt, letting them collect and pile up at her belly, where the shirt was tucked into her elastic pants. She went behind the counter and was desperately grabbing more items when the door chimed.

"Shoplifter?" The officer voice sounded bored until he took quick stock of the store. "What's going on in here?"

"This girl," the clerk said, pointing at Violet. "There's something wrong with her. She's just going nuts." A terrified giggle escaped his throat.

The officer rounded the corner toward Violet. "You," he said, a hand on his hip. "Stay where you are. Put your hands up."

Violet froze for a second. She was caught and needed to find a way out—with her food. Thinking fast, she bolted in the other direction, running smack into a glass freezer door. The chips crunched in her shirt, the bag busting and an orange cloud of dust exploding in her face and dirtying her glasses. The officer gained on her immediately, pulling her arms behind her.

"You're under arrest for shoplifting and for attempted evasion of an officer of the law. You have the right to remain silent . . ." The officer went on, but Violet was frantically trying to fight him off. She was howling, not just because she was in trouble, but because he was going to *take away her food*. She yelled and tried to head butt the officer from behind.

"You don't want to add battery of an officer to the list of things you've done today, do you?" The officer was gentle with her but firmly led her to his squad car.

The ringing phone awoke Ian at one a.m. Something had to be wrong. His mind immediately went to Mitchell. What kind of trouble had his son gotten into?

"Mr. Durkin?"

"Yes," Ian said.

"I'm calling from the city police department," the man said. "We have your daughter, Violet, in custody."

Ian shot straight up in bed. "What?"

"We got a call that there was a shoplifter at the convenience store. When I arrived on the scene, she had all of her clothes stuffed with food, and she had attacked the clerk, who said it was the second time she'd been there tonight. When I approached her, she ran, and then she tried to escape. She's being held on charges of shoplifting, evading arrest, and attempted assault of an officer. I can tell that she maybe has some problems, so I'll drop the charges if you come get her right now, pay for the stolen merchandise, and assure me we'll never see her again downtown."

"Thank you, officer," Ian said, breathless with relief. Samantha sat up and her eyes got wide at the word "officer." "I'll be there as soon as I can."

"What's going on?" Samantha cried as soon as Ian hung up the phone.

"Violet is in custody—" Ian started.

"Violet?" Samantha exclaimed. "That's impossible."

"It's happening. She must have snuck out. I don't know.

The officer is going to drop charges if I get her now." Ian stood and pulled on a pair of athletic shorts that were lying on the floor beside the bed.

"Should I come with you?" Samantha asked.

"Just stay here. We'll be back in a little while."

...

"What did you do, Violet? What happened?" Samantha leaned toward her daughter on the couch. Ian had just brought her home, and Samantha couldn't keep her cool. She went into interrogation mode.

"I didn't do anything wrong!" Violet protested. "The police officer was mean!"

"He wasn't mean, Violet. He let you go. You could have gone to jail. You stole! And you snuck out of the house!"

"Screw you, Mom!" Violet cried out. She stood and pushed her mother before running toward the stairs. Samantha was hot on her heels until Violet reached her bedroom door. She slammed it in her mother's face, and when Samantha tried to block the door, her finger got caught in the hinge. The bones on her right ring finger crunched, reminding Violet of the chips that had exploded in her face, and causing another howling meltdown on the other side of the door.

"Shit!" Samantha yelled, her voice joining the chorus of her daughter's hapless sobs. Samantha slid to the floor, unable to do anything but repeat the expletive and examine her hand. Her fingernail was bloody and the bone was crooked. Her hands shook, and as the gravity of the evening hit her physically, the rest of her body began to tremble.

"Are you okay?" Ian asked, rushing over to his wife.

"My finger is broken," Samantha said. She cradled that hand with her other one, looking at Ian with the lack of comprehension that comes with sudden injury. Surprising both of them, she doubled over with laughter, collapsing into the fetal position on the hardwood floor of the hallway. Tears began falling down her cheeks through her cackle, and she wasn't sure if she could feel anything at all anymore.

"Sam?" Ian said cautiously, bending toward his wife.

"Do we have any popsicles?" Samantha asked, sounding perfectly capable just as suddenly as she had turned hysterical moments earlier. "I'm going to have to set this."

Ian nodded. "I'll go grab the sticks."

"I guess we're going to have to set up guard," Samantha said to Ian's back. He paused on the stairwell. "Do you want the first night shift, or should I take it?"

Ian turned, his face looking older than she recalled it looking earlier that day. "I'll take it. I can pull the recliner out of the bedroom and sit out here tonight. I have to work in the morning, so you'll have the day shift."

"Deal," Samantha agreed, wearily rising and following Ian to the kitchen. It was going to be a long week.

· · ·

The next morning, Samantha was waiting for Violet in the kitchen when she came downstairs. Violet's face was downcast and guarded, and Samantha felt a crumbling inside her. Adult or not, Violet was still a child. A child with a rare disability she hadn't asked for, a life that would never be normal.

"Hey, Vi," Samantha said, her voice gentle. "Ready for breakfast?"

"Yes, please," Violet said, taking her seat at the dining table. She looked at Samantha timidly.

"We'll get through this, honey," Samantha said. Careful not to move her finger, set and taped against two popsicle sticks, she brought granola and yogurt to the table and sat next to her daughter. Everything seemed grotesquely normal, and it filled Samantha with a sense of dread.

That night, Samantha got Violet to bed at her normal time, and Ian took his post at Violet's door.

"Goodnight, sweetheart. Thank you." Samantha ran her fingers through Ian's hair.

"Good thing I'm a light sleeper," Ian joked, settling into the chair with a book. "Don't worry about it, Sam. I've got this."

CHAPTER 10

"Sheila will be here soon," Ian called out to his daughter and wife.

After they'd signed the necessary paperwork, Sheila, their social worker, had sat down with Violet and her parents to discuss the change. Everyone explained to Violet that she was a good girl and that her parents just wanted her to stay somewhere where she would be happy and safe, and where she could reach her full potential. While Violet seemed to understand during their conversation with Sheila, now that Sunday had arrived, Violet was unhappy with the arrangement.

"Mom, I promise I'll be a good girl," Violet cried, sitting on her bed while Samantha gathered the last of her things into a piece of luggage. "I promise. I won't sneak out. I won't leave Grammy and Pops. I won't steal. I will take my medicine."

Samantha's heart broke at her daughter's tearful pleas. She sat down on the bed and took Violet's hand between both of hers. "Vi, this has nothing to do with you being good. Remember when we talked about that on Friday? This is kind of like going away to college. Your brothers didn't go away to college because we didn't want them to live with us anymore—they went away because it was the best place for them to be."

"But Mitchell left college," Violet argued. "It wasn't the best place for him. What if that happens to me? What if I try to come home, and you don't let me, like you didn't let Mitch come home after my graduation party? I don't have any friends that I can go live with, like Mitch does. What will happen to me?" Violet's voice was rising, her face wretched with anxiety.

"Violet, Mitchell's situation was very different than yours. Mitchell wasn't making good choices, and he *chose* not to come home. He—" Samantha paused. Her middle son was such a riddle that she wasn't even sure how to explain him to herself, much less to her daughter. She could see where Violet would get confused by the analogy to Mitchell's departure, but it was the best thing that she had. Samantha knew that she needed to hold it together, for Violet's sake, but all she wanted to do was join her daughter under the covers and hide. She took a deep breath.

"Violet, we're not sending you away. We're trying to work with people so that you can live in a place where you're happy. Dad and I want the best life for you, just like we want the best for your brothers. We make choices in your best interest, just like we tried to do for Mitchell. If you're unhappy where you go, and it's legitimate, we'll investigate and find a better place for you. Mitchell's unhappiness was not legitimate. He wasn't making good choices and got frustrated when the consequences caught up with him. Your life and his life are very different, and I can assure you that your father and I will take every step to defend you and to make sure that your life works. Do you understand what I'm saying?"

Violet nodded calmly, looking deeply into her mother's eyes.

Just then, Ian walked into Violet's bedroom. "Girls, Sheila will . . ." he trailed off. "What's going on?" He furrowed his brow as he took a seat on the bed with his wife and daughter.

"Mom says that where I go will be fun and that I will have a happier life." Violet looked at her father, her earnest words ringing. In her simple language, she'd managed to speak every hope that her parents had for her.

"Of course we aren't trying to get rid of you. Remember when we talked to Sheila, and she helped us explain what's going on?" Ian leaned into his daughter. He could feel Samantha's intense emotion behind him and knew that he should continue the conversation with Violet.

Violet nodded again. "Will you come see me?"

"Of course," Ian responded, putting his hand on her shoulder. "We want to give you a few days to get settled in, but we will come and see you as much as we can." Although he planned to see or call her every day, he didn't want to make that promise, just in case there was a day they couldn't make it. "Remember, Violet," Ian continued, "this is temporary. We will reevaluate everything soon." He leaned in and hugged his daughter.

"We love you so much and will miss you, but we all have to be brave right now, because you're an adult."

Violet leaned into the hug. "I love you, too."

The sound of the doorbell broke their embrace, and Ian led Violet downstairs to greet Sheila while Samantha finished gathering Violet's things.

"Hey, Violet." Sheila's tone was soft. She reached over to embrace the girl, and Violet gave her a furious hug in return. "Are you ready to go, sweetie?"

Violet nodded. "Just waiting for my stuff."

Sheila glanced over at Ian. He rubbed his red eyes with his fingers and smiled at her. "How are you today?" she asked.

"I'm excited for Violet to see her new house. I'm only sad because my little girl is all grown up," he said, putting on a smile and placing his arm around his daughter.

Samantha came downstairs, balancing a small suitcase and a two-inch binder, into which she'd placed all of Violet's necessary medical information and general information about Prader-Willi Syndrome, just in case the residential facility wasn't as familiar as they needed to be with Violet's condition.

"Hi, Sheila," she called out, her voice heavier than she'd intended.

"Hello, Samantha. Are these the last of Violet's things?" Sheila asked, collecting the luggage and binder and gesturing to the two suitcases by the door.

"They are," Samantha said.

"Well, I'm going to load the car. The three of you should have some time together," Sheila said. She balanced the smaller suitcase on top of one of the rolling bags and pushed the binder under her arm.

"We've had time. Let's go," Violet said, looking Sheila right in the eye.

Sheila looked back at the Durkins, trying to read their cues as to what she should do next. Ian nodded, and Samantha looked at her daughter with tears in her eyes. Violet had decided to be brave and get the trip out of the way. Samantha was relieved that Violet bought into the need for residential care but was heartbroken that she'd resolved to leave so quickly.

"We'll walk you out, Vi." Ian turned to Samantha, and the three of them followed Sheila to her sedan. They loaded up the car, and with hugs and an "I love you" whispered into Violet's cheek, their daughter was gone.

Samantha and Ian stood in their driveway, watching Sheila's powder blue hybrid turn left at the stop sign and then fade away.

"So this is what an empty nest is like," Samantha remarked to Ian, stepping closer to him. He grabbed her hand and turned to her with a sad smile.

"This is the way things have to be, Sam. The natural order. Children grow up and leave their parents behind for pursuit of their own best interests," Ian said, still looking toward the end of their block.

"Don't give me your psychobabble, Ian," Samantha said sharply. "I know that, logically. I just can't help but feel that we have given her away."

Ian turned to look at his wife, and it seemed as though all of the white noise that had filled his brain was now gone. He was able to see the woman he had married—for better or worse. His heart swelled with gratitude that despite thirty years of marriage, she still called him out when he needed it. That tough woman who'd crashed through the glass ceiling of her career completed him, as a person and as a parenting team. "You're right, Sam. I'm trying to make this intellectual because I just want my baby back. But that's not realistic. The past few months have shown that we just can't do this. I trust Sheila. She isn't going to let us down. Besides, it's only two weeks. If it isn't working, we can pull her out. She's close."

Samantha sighed. "You're right. Let's go inside." She

led her husband back into the house, where the most quiet and normal Sunday evening they'd ever had awaited them.

...

"I think it's going to work out well." Sheila's voice was optimistic on the phone with Samantha the following morning. "They're working with an authority on Prader-Willi treatment and looking forward to having Violet in placement."

"Wait, they don't have any experiences with Prader-Willi?" Samantha exclaimed. "Sheila, you assured us—"

"I assured you that I would find a home that would work for Violet. This place is working with the experts to make a community, much like the one in Wisconsin that I discussed with you. They're building the program, and Violet gets to be on the ground floor of that. That's groundbreaking for our state."

"My daughter is not a guinea pig!" Samantha said.

"Of course she isn't, Sam," Sheila said reassuringly. "She is the first patient who will benefit from the knowledge they've gained."

Samantha bristled but chose to move on. "How did she do when you dropped her off?"

"She was shy at first, but that's to be expected. I showed her to her room. She has a roommate, an adorable girl about her own age."

"Does the girl also have Prader-Willi?" Samantha asked.

"She doesn't. I can't discuss her condition with you, as I don't know anything about her. I'm sure that you can get more information when you go visit Violet later this week."

"We'll be visiting Violet on Wednesday," Samantha curtly responded. "Have you heard anything from the funding agency?"

"The emergency funding is in place, obviously. Due to Violet's tumultuous past few months, I don't anticipate continued funding here to be an issue. However, we'll know in about a week." Sheila kept her voice steady.

"Continued funding isn't what we talked about. You said that we had a good shot of trying to get Violet into PWHO in Wisconsin. This was supposed to be a temporary placement," Samantha said. She couldn't help feeling swindled.

"Go visit her," Sheila said. "If you feel iffy about the placement, we'll make a new plan. This is a difficult adjustment for parents. We all want what's best for Violet. I promise."

. . .

"If we hurry, we'll be there at two," Samantha said, buckling her seatbelt. She and Ian had both taken half days at work to visit Violet, and Samantha was excited to see Violet again. She'd visited on three different days the week before, but this was only the second time that she and Ian were able to visit Violet together. Violet had been at the facility for two weeks, and the last time Samantha had visited, she'd been struck by how unenthusiastic her daughter seemed. Her normally sparkling green eyes were dim, even though Violet said things were "okay." Samantha told herself to be patient, that this was a big transition, albeit a temporary one, and she was feeling almost desperate for reassurance that Violet was okay.

"The facility is only half an hour away," Ian responded,

trying to keep his cool amid his wife's impatience. He was in the same place, mentally and emotionally as Samantha. He'd gotten away from work as quickly as he could, and the night before was filled with sleeplessness and anxiety about what the day would bring.

Both Durkins forgot how much easier traffic was to negotiate in the middle of the day, and only twenty-two minutes later, Ian and Samantha pulled into the parking lot of the facility.

As they walked into the older building, Ian was struck by the facility's resemblance to the nursing home where he'd worked during his medical residency. He'd chosen an older home, one that wasn't fancy, because he knew the patients there needed mental health care more than other patients in a rehab center. He felt like he could save the world then, and the memory of his former feeling of invincibility made him wince when he realized that his own child was in a similar facility—somewhere people came to die.

After signing in, Samantha and Ian were led to the common room, where patients were allowed to visit with their families. Violet was sitting on a couch in the corner, staring at the cartoons on the television.

"Hey, baby!" Samantha's voice was light—she put on her sunniest smile for her daughter.

Violet looked up at her parents with dull eyes. "Hello," she said coldly.

Ian hugged his daughter, noting how much fleshier her arms and back had become. "How are you, angel?"

"You lied! This isn't like going away to college! This is awful. Why did you throw me away?" Violet's eyes filled with tears.

"We haven't. We just want you to get the help you need, sweetheart." Ian's eyes reflected his daughter's pain.

Violet's eyes turned spiteful. Knowing this would provoke her dad, she said, "Well, everyone is *very* helpful. I get to watch TV and eat whatever I want whenever I'm hungry."

Ian's chest tightened with Violet's lie. "What do you mean, Vi? What's your schedule like here?"

Violet shrugged and directed her attention back to the television. "Seriously, just leave me here. I'm way happier than I could ever be at home, and I don't want you to come visit anymore."

Ian was moved to action. He needed to take a look at Violet's medical charts, talk with the doctors who were treating her, to see exactly what was going on.

"I'm going to talk to the doctor. I'll be right back." He patted Violet's knee before making his way across the fluorescent-lit room to the offices around the corner.

"Hi. I'm Dr. Durkin, Violet's father. Are her doctors around today?"

The receptionist looked up. "Yes, but I think they're very busy."

Ian was infuriated at her response. "Well, I'd like to talk to them. In the meantime, I'd like to take a look at her chart."

The receptionist said, "I'm sorry Dr. Durkin. I'm not allowed to just hand you her chart. You're going to have to wait for the doctor. I'll tell him you want to see him."

Ian sat in the lobby, increasingly impatient. After ten minutes, he walked back up to the receptionist. "I need to talk to Dr. Phelan. Now. I'll go back there and find him myself if I have to. *I will* speak with Violet's doctor today.

It's my right as her legal guardian." Ian's voice shook with anger, and the receptionist stared at him for a long moment before standing and leaving the room.

A few minutes later, she returned with Dr. Phelan, who asked the receptionist for Violet's chart. He led Ian down a dim hallway and turned into a conference room. Dr. Phelan sat across from Ian at an oval table and handed Ian the chart.

"You'll see that we're doing the best we can for her," Dr. Phelan said, "the way we do for all of our clients."

Without replying, Ian dove into the doctor's notes. When he reached her daily check-up, he stopped, shocked. He looked again to check his math. Yes. His daughter had ballooned twenty-five pounds in less than two weeks. Ian put his face into his hands. Clearly, they had no idea how to treat Violet here. He knew that he and Samantha couldn't take care of her like she needed, but she would die here, soon and miserably, if they didn't get her the help she needed.

"What seems to be the problem, Dr. Durkin?" Dr. Phelan asked.

"Violet hasn't quite been here for two weeks, and already she's gained twenty five pounds," Ian said, narrowing his eyes at the doctor. "Could you explain how you're building a successful program for patients with Prader-Willi Syndrome if your first patient is seeing that kind of weight gain in two weeks?"

Dr. Phelan looked at the chart that Ian handed back to him. "Weight gain isn't uncommon when medications have been changed. As a psychiatrist, you should know that."

"Her medication has been changed?" Ian exclaimed.

"That's *illegal*. We are Violet's guardians, and no medication changes can be made without our expressed consent," He hadn't gotten that far into her chart and was furious that such a decision had been made without discussing it with either him or Samantha. "Have you even consulted with Dr. Kraemer?"

Dr. Phelan looked confused. "Was he Violet's psychiatrist before?"

"Yes! He was! He has been treating Violet since she was thirteen years old! Certainly, his opinion should be taken into consideration before a medication change."

"Dr. Durkin, respectfully, the cocktail that Dr. Kraemer had Violet on wasn't effective, or she wouldn't be here. As you know, we are working with an authority on Prader-Willi Syndrome to build a program for Prader-Willi here. Violet is our first patient. Please be patient with us as we—"

Ian cut the doctor off. "I'd be willing to be patient if you were actually *treating* Violet. This weight gain indicates that you are not. Would you mind explaining your treatment plan for Violet?"

"We have scheduled meals for everyone. We take care to ensure that Violet can't access our kitchen. We offer a gym for Violet to do daily workouts, but we can't force her to do any of that if she chooses not to," Dr. Phelan said, defensively.

"You *have* to force her to do these things, to keep her alive! And how do you ensure that she won't access the kitchen? Do you have locks?" Ian asked.

"We can't lock our kitchen," Dr. Phelan said, as if he were talking to a child. "That's a human rights violation according to our accreditation. However, we ensure that

Violet gets one portion of everything at meal times. Most of our patients maintain a healthy weight with our meals, so I don't understand the weight gain any more than you do."

"Food isn't the only issue." Ian lowered his head to his hands and squeezed his temples. "Listen, this just isn't going to work. I'm withdrawing Violet from your facility today. Please get the paperwork in order."

Ian was close to tears. The one option—the one thing that had given Ian and Samantha a glimmer of hope—was crashing down around him.

• • •

On the ride home, Violet was silent in the backseat, staring out the window. Samantha hadn't witnessed Ian's impassioned defense of Violet, but she knew that things were awful from her daughter's demeanor.

"You just wait until I tell Sheila," Samantha said quietly to Ian. "She'll regret ever betraying our trust."

"She talked a good game for someone who doesn't know anything about Prader-Willi," Ian said back, just as quietly. "Right now, I'm done with the state. It's time to discuss possible options with Mrs. Posey."

Samantha nodded. She and Ian had told Mrs. Posey of Violet's turmoil this summer, and she had reassured the Durkins that she would help in any way she could. From the car, Samantha emailed her assistant to say she'd be working from home the rest of the week, dreading what that time might look like.

The family pulled into their garage, and Ian silently took Violet's bags from the trunk.

"We're happy that you're home again, Violet," Samantha

said, putting her arm around her daughter and leading her into the house.

"I'm tired," Violet said, walking ahead of her mother.

Samantha followed Violet to her bedroom, where she tucked into her bed.

"Violet, will you miss it there?" she asked, smoothing her daughter's hair behind her ears.

"I'll only miss my roommate, Jennifer," Violet said.

"Tell me about her," Samantha said.

"She was really pretty. She had autism and didn't talk much," Violet replied. "Her mother sent her care packages all the time. She got two while I was there. Homemade cookies and lots of candy. Jennifer shared with me, although sometimes I took more after she was asleep."

Samantha's stomach sank. That explained why Violet's face looked rounder than it had just days earlier. That facility was probably okay for patients with different special needs, but the staff had no idea how Prader-Willi worked.

"All right, baby. You get some rest. I'll be here when you wake up," Samantha said, patting her daughter's head and twisting the external deadbolt that she and Ian had installed on Violet's door while she was away—just in case. Violet needed to sleep, and hopefully when she woke, the whole ordeal would just seem like a bad dream. Samantha made her way downstairs, where she found Ian in his home office.

"Now, what's going on?" she asked him.

"Violet gained twenty-five pounds in two weeks. Are you kidding me? I can't believe that we were dumb enough to just let her go wherever the state decided that she should. I can't believe that we didn't investigate more fully," Ian said angrily. He didn't look away from the computer screen.

"We were out of options," Samantha countered. "We thought we could trust her."

"I'm going to call Mrs. Posey," Ian was resolute. "She's going to help us. She has to."

"Have you given any more thought to PWHO in Wisconsin?" Samantha asked carefully. "From what I understand, it's the best."

"That's what Sheila mentioned, so I'm skeptical. I'd like to check it out, though. I don't know what we're going to do with Violet in the meantime. We're just back to square one, although I'd rather live in a cardboard box than put her anywhere like that again," Ian said. "I'm going to call Mrs. Posey. Then, I'm going to call my mother and see if she can spend next week here with Violet. *Then* I'm going to call Dr. Kraemer to discuss the changes that were made to Violet's medication. You start the research on other facilities for us to check out in person. Start with PWHO, if you'd like, but please search thoroughly," Ian said. He turned his back to Samantha and dialed the phone.

Samantha blinked. Rarely was Ian more action oriented than she was, and seeing him this way brought her a sense of comfort.

"Mrs. Posey," a smooth voice answered.

"Hi, Mrs. Posey, this is Ian Durkin. How are you?"

"I'm well, Ian. How is our sweet girl?"

"She's not well, actually," Ian said, feeling sick. "We pulled her from the residential facility today because with her condition, the treatment that she was receiving was not meeting her needs; it was just not an appropriate placement. They knew little about Prader-Willi."

"Oh my. I'm so sorry to hear that." Mrs. Posey's voice broke with emotion.

"Yes, me too. Mrs. Posey, you said that if we ever needed your help, just to let you know. Well, we do now. We were working with a social worker who recommended this place and got us emergency funding. She set things up so that Violet's funding would go from an emergency placement to a regular full-funded placement, but at the same facility. Obviously, that's not going to work. I know that there are options through the school board." Ian said.

"I see, and there are options, Ian. Just in case we came to this, I've done some research on potential options for Violet, and the only place that I can find that seems to know as much about Prader-Willi as you do is in Wisconsin." Mrs. Posey said, thoughtfully.

"The social worker with the state recommended the same place. Apparently it has a very good reputation." Ian sighed, curious about the draw that this place held.

"My first recommendation is to stay on the educational track, try to pursue placement that way, and to discontinue contact with Sheila for now. The state is a different system. Start researching facilities where you'd like Violet placed. Go check out PWHO in Wisconsin, and if you think it will be a fit, let me know. We need to have a facility in mind before we're granted your funding so that I can push it through to get it approved." Mrs. Posey's voice was warm with concern, but bright with hope. She always wanted to see Violet win.

"Also," Mrs. Posey continued, "I need you and Sam to get together all the documentation you can of Violet's syndrome and the effects it's had on your lives. You two should also write letters about her treatment at the facility she just left. Get notes from her doctors, psychiatrists, your parents . . . Any and every piece of information that you can arm me with will be helpful." Mrs. Posey said. After that, we need to call an IEP team meeting to review all the information and discuss the possibility of placement. Then the question will be where."

"I will," Ian replied. "Thank you, Mrs. Posey. We don't know what we'd do without you." He hung up the phone feeling heard for the first time in a long time. Finally, someone else seemed to understand the gravity of Violet's situation. It wasn't just about finding a babysitter for their daughter; it was about finding a place where Violet could be happy and fulfilled. He picked up the phone to make his other phone calls, optimistic that they were finally doing the *right* thing for Violet, as opposed to just doing *something.*

CHAPTER 11

Ian's mother could only spend a week with Violet, so the following two weeks involved Samantha and Ian taking turns working from home and supervising their daughter, as well as gathering the required paperwork, attending the formal IEP meeting, and reviewing all of Violet's progress. Finally, they got a recommendation for a specific residential placement at Prader-Willi Homes of Oconomowoc.

Violet's attitude didn't improve the stressful situation. Dr. Kraemer had placed Violet back on her medication, but the abrupt changes had been too much for her. Samantha's anxiety was at an all-time high after continually finding Violet's hair in bloody clumps in the shower drain and new scabs on Violet's body. Samantha could do nothing to alleviate Violet's anxiety except to sleep with her daughter at night. Violet found comfort in her mother's warmth behind her, and Samantha could prevent Violet from getting out of bed for any reason other than using the bathroom. The co-sleeping was working well for Violet, but Samantha was exhausted. Every time the bed shifted under Violet's considerable weight, Samantha jolted awake with a feeling like she was falling.

In the absence of sleep, Samantha found herself repeatedly wandering over to the PWHO website. She felt like a girl shopping for engagement rings, returning to the same bookmarked page over and over even though her boyfriend hadn't yet proposed.

The line at the top of the website, "Providing Homes with a Heart," almost made Samantha swoon. The scrapbook feel of the site and the pictures of happy residents tugged at Samantha's heartstrings. She'd been burned by a residential facility before and didn't want to get her hopes up, but still, she was drawn to PWHO. They had dealt exclusively with Prader-Willi Syndrome for over thirty-five years. They would look out for Violet's best interest because they understood the treatment that her syndrome required. On a whim, Samantha picked up her office phone and dialed the number to the admissions office. The worst thing that would happen was that whoever answered the phone would be rude or unknowledgeable, and she figured it was better to know that now than when the funding was approved and they were in search of a place for Violet to live.

"Prader-Willi Homes of Oconomowoc, this is Marilyn." The pleasant voice rang in Samantha ear.

Samantha burst into tears. She didn't see them coming enough to fight them off and struggled to introduce herself through the bizarre torrent. "I'm so sorry," she said in between sobs. "I never do this, I . . . My name is Samantha Durkin, and I'm calling about my daughter, Violet."

"It's okay, Samantha. This is obviously a hard phone call to make and a difficult time for you and your family. Take your time." Marilyn's voice was reassuring. "I'm the admissions director here at PWHO, so you're talking to the right person. I'll be happy to answer any of your questions about our facility."

"That's wonderful," Samantha said, trying to pull herself together. She sniffed. "My daughter, Violet, just can't live at home anymore. I hate that, but it's true." In the nearly two hours that followed, Samantha summarized Violet's life, culminating with the drama of the last few months and their terrible experience with the in-state residential facility. "We're at the end of our rope, waiting for funding to come through from the state education board and trying to find a place where our daughter will not only be well taken care of but also have the potential to have a happy life."

"Samantha, your concerns are very important to me, and I understand how deeply you want what's best for Violet. The bad experience that you had with a residential facility, I'm guessing it was one that didn't specialize in Prader-Willi Syndrome?" Marilyn asked.

"Right. They didn't know much about Prader-Willi. She was rooming with a girl with autism. The girl's parents sent care packages almost every day, full of cookies and candy. Violet destroyed those. She gained twenty-five pounds in two weeks. The staff didn't understand why, because they said they'd kept her from food," Samantha said shakily.

"Well, Prader-Willi Syndrome is paradoxical in many ways. Not only is there the increased appetite due to the hypothalamic dysfunction, but there is also the unique feature of reduced metabolic functioning. I can understand why Violet gained so much weight in such a short amount of time if her eating went unchecked," Marilyn said. And while it was nothing that Samantha didn't know, the fact that someone was telling her about it instead of the other way around comforted her.

"How are you different?" Samantha asked quietly.

"Well, we understand Prader-Willi Syndrome and have been working for a long time with people who have it. It's such a rare syndrome that we find there is a lot of misinformation circulating out there. From the day a person arrives here, we—along with our house managers, the group home direct treatment teams, clinical coordinators, staff psychiatrist, our nurses, the parents, and other professionals who previously worked with our residents—create an Individual Service Plan, or ISP. In the home, we offer daily group sessions with the house manager and have house motivational systems to encourage healthy behaviors and habits, as well as programs to improve self-image, teach skills in all areas of daily living, and help develop positive social interaction skills. We provide individual, group, and family therapy. Therapy is provided by the clinical coordinator, who is also the case manager and the primary contact for the family when a person comes to placement. We also have a vocational program, where our residents go into the community and have jobs and responsibilities. Additionally, our residents receive twenty-four-hour awake supervision from our staff, all of whom are trained in the intricacies of Prader-Willi Syndrome and the therapeutic approaches effective with people who have been diagnosed with it."

Samantha was refreshed by Marilyn's answers.

"Let me ask you a question, Samantha," Marilyn said. "What has gotten you to this point? Was Violet at home until recently?"

Samantha unloaded, telling Marilyn about Violet's summer from hell: how everything looked up in June, but then she hurt herself, and was hospitalized for two weeks before staying with her grandparents for the day, an arrangement that only lasted six weeks, until Violet ran away from their house and her parents caught her stealing from her grandparents. She continued by telling Marilyn how Violet was home for a bit, then snuck out of the house and was arrested for stealing food at a corner store, then went to residential treatment for two weeks, and then was pulled back home. Samantha concluded the saga by explaining that the decision to place their daughter in residential care wasn't their first choice, and they weren't looking for a way out of her life, but a way back in. "I just want to be her mother again, not her prison guard." The tears settled in again, but this time Samantha didn't even try to compose herself. She let them flow in fat drops down her cheeks, relieved that she could talk to someone who understood what Violet was like.

"What a hard road," Marilyn said. "You seem to have handled it with grit and grace, and I respect you for that. This is never any parent's first choice, but the reality is that residential facilities are needed. Otherwise, we wouldn't be here. Group home residential facilities are considered less restrictive because they are community based. Here's what I would like to do. Could you and your husband come to Oconomowoc for a visit? I'd like to show you our program first hand."

Samantha stopped. An offer to see the facility? She couldn't believe it. "We will have to bring Violet with us," she said. While thrilled by the offer, she was trying to name every impediment to the plan in her head, just so she didn't get her hopes crushed again.

"Of course! Bring Violet so we can meet her! That's even better!" Marilyn said.

Samantha was so grateful for Marilyn's kind words that she smiled through her tears. "I'll talk it over with my husband, but I'm sure we can make something work. Thank you, Marilyn, for everything."

Samantha hung up the phone and stared out the window. Her daughter could have a place in the world—a place where she could flourish.

Violet's medication switches were making her more tired than usual, and she was already in bed when Samantha got home that night. Ian was in the living room with his feet up and a documentary on the History channel playing quietly on the television.

"Honey, I'm home," Samantha said, quietly, coming around to have a seat next to him.

"How was your day?" Ian asked, his eyes tired.

"It was actually really good," Samantha said, recounting her experience on the phone with Marilyn from PWHO and looking into Ian's eyes to gauge his reaction. "She said to come visit—that'd they'd love to meet Violet."

Ian looked at her. "We need to go out there anyway, but they had that kind of attitude?" His eyes were surprised.

"Yes. And for once, someone was making comments about Violet's syndrome that were right on. I didn't have to correct her or explain anything," Samantha said.

"Well, that's a nice change of pace."

"I'll call Marilyn tomorrow to see when we can tour the facility. Assuming it's as good as it sounds, I want to get Violet on that list so if there's an opening, it's hers," Samantha said. She had no idea if there was an opening at PWHO, or if there was a waiting list, but it just seemed logical that there might be, and it was a contingency for which she wanted to prepare.

Ian finally looked over to Samantha. "Do you think Violet will ever be happy? Even with a placement? What if it's like the last place?"

"We won't send her anywhere like the last place, because we're in charge this time. Let's at least go visit PWHO and see what they have to offer," Samantha said, putting her hand on Ian's cheek.

"Sounds good," Ian responded. "Let's find something for our girl."

CHAPTER 12

Violet was convinced that her parents were just trying to get rid of her again. She'd just gotten out of the hellhole where they'd made her stay before when they loaded her up in their SUV and drove hours away from their home in the city to the middle-of-nowhere-Wisconsin. They spoke to her with big eyes and excited voices, but she knew that only meant that they were feigning excitement so that they could leave her in the worst version of a nightmare: a place where they would feed her too much or too little, and no one would talk to her.

Violet plopped herself on the unoccupied queen bed of their hotel room and sighed dramatically. She hated everything about her Prader-Willi. It didn't make her special or interesting; it only made her hungry and easily annoyed. Everyone said they just wanted her to be happy, that they wanted the best life for her, but she didn't see where that would ever be a possibility. She didn't sign up for Prader-Willi, but it ruled her life. Every decision was driven by finding her next meal. She just wanted to live a *normal* life. She wanted to go away to college, to get married, and to have babies. She wanted to do everything that girls did on TV, everything that she *should* have been able to do, but the only thing she could do was be locked away from everything she knew.

The chatter of the news that her father was watching faded as she buried her face into the pillow. The pillowcase scratched the sides of her cheek a little, and she breathed in the sanitary smell of the commercial laundry detergent. She exhaled, then filled her lungs again when she realized that deep breathing wasn't going to fix anything. She screamed, the loud vocal escape making her throat scratchy, and her breath stretched into the pillow and made her face warm and moist.

Ian jumped from his bed and rushed over to his daughter. He grabbed her shoulders gently. "Violet, Violet," he repeated, turning her around so that her face was no longer buried in the pillow. She avoided eye contact with her father, continuing to howl in the hotel room. "Violet, I'm here. I'm here, baby." He smoothed her hair behind her ears, the screams quieting to whimpers, and Ian pulled his daughter into his chest. Her body heaved with sobs as he rubbed her back soothingly.

"Baby, it's okay. It's okay. I'm here," he said quietly into his daughter's hair. Violet's chest rose with a deep breath, and Ian could almost *feel* something rattle inside of her. His whole family was broken. None of them could grasp onto that rattling piece and put it back again. The residential care facility they were visiting the next day was their last hope for any one of them to become whole again. While Violet was the only one who acted on her anxiety, her sobs echoed inside the empty space of Ian's chest.

"Why are you getting rid of me again?" Violet pleaded as she looked up at her father. Her green eyes shone bright with tears, turning them almost brown, matching the scattering of freckles across her nose.

"Violet, we never want to get rid of you. We just want you to be happy." Ian's voice broke with emotion.

"I can't be happy, Dad." Violet pulled away, looking at him solemnly. "I can't be happy because I didn't ask to have Prader-Willi. I don't want to be this way. I want to go to college. I want to get married and have babies. I want to be pretty and be a grown-up like Luke and Mitch."

Ian had to work to prevent a flinch when Violet compared her life to the lives of her brothers. "You are pretty, and you are grown up," he reassured her. "This could be the place where you're allowed to do all of that. This is a program designed for people who didn't ask for Prader-Willi. You could have a job, make friends, and live in a supportive environment. Nothing is for sure yet, Violet. We're all going to look at this place tomorrow. We will all decide if you go there. Not like last time."

Violet blinked at him, acknowledging his statement, even if her trust in her father was still shaken.

Ian's heart was heavy with all the conversations that he couldn't have with his daughter. She was a bright girl—people with Prader-Willi often were far lower functioning than she was—but she wasn't capable of having the kinds of discussions that decisions like this warranted. While he and Samantha would never make any decision that they absolutely didn't believe was right for their child, she could only see their actions as a move against her. It would always be a conversation that Violet had with herself and one he was unpacking in his soul. He decided to see if he could distract her from the topic, at least until Samantha got back from picking up dinner.

"Do you want the remote?" Ian tried to smile as he

reached over to the nightstand that separated the two beds.

Violet smiled and nodded; her eyes didn't betray a moment of her prior emotional outburst. Ian placed the remote in his daughter's lap and leaned against the headboard of the bed. Violet leaned over to her father, and he put his arm around her, looking down at her fine brown waves in the crook of his arm. Although Violet's outbursts were sudden and sometimes extreme, she often forgot them as quickly as they came on. Ian tried to remind himself that he was lucky his eighteen-year-old daughter would still cuddle with him and watch TV. It had been years since either of his sons had voluntarily hugged him, much less settled in for a half-hour show under his arm.

"Dad, is it time for dinner yet?" Violet asked, trying to keep her voice casual. She glanced at the digital clock on the cable box in the hotel. It read five-thirty, which was dinnertime on the schedule that Ian and Samantha had rebuilt in the few weeks that Violet had been back home.

"Mom's on her way, sweetheart," Ian said. "Remember, she went out to get us sandwiches?"

"Yeah. Will she remember to put all the veggies on my sandwich? Spinach, tomatoes, onions, banana peppers, bell peppers . . ." Violet yawned. In the past few weeks, she'd started going to bed right after dinner. Although her medication transition was now complete, her body had adjusted to the habit, and her eyes were starting to feel heavy.

"And pickles. We know what you like, sweetie. I promise that she'll be back here soon with a sandwich stuffed with every veggie they have. Mom has never let you down before." The words echoed in the silence that followed

Ian's words, haunting him. Samantha had tried her best, they both had, but Ian wasn't sure that was a fair statement to make to his daughter. He was glad she seemed to ignore it, and he tried to focus on the television show. A minute later, the electronic key beeped in the door, and Ian breathed a silent sigh of relief that his wife was back with dinner.

"Who's hungry?" Samantha called as she walked into the room with two plastic bags hanging from her hands. She could feel her daughter's eyes following the bags as she walked to the table. "Sweetie, let me get you set up here," she said.

The sound of the waxed paper unfolding was almost too much for Violet. Her mouth watered, and she rose from bed and stood behind her mother. As soon as Samantha stepped out of the way, Violet was in the chair and shoving the sandwich in her mouth.

"Slow down, sweetie." Samantha put a hand on her daughter's shoulder. This was a delicate point for Violet, but she didn't want to see her daughter choke. "No one is going to take it away from you."

"Why are you always picking on me?" Violet burst out. Her anxiety was high anyway, and even though her mother was trying to keep her tone light, the tension with her parents completely set her on edge. "No one says anything to you when you're eating, Mom. Why do you watch me like a hawk? I'm so damn tired of being treated this way!" Violet could feel her heart beating in her throat. She set down her sandwich and took a deep breath. The rage subsided as quickly as it came on. *It's because I'm bad,* she thought, *That's why they're trying to get rid of me. That's why we're here in the first place. I don't want to be bad! I want to be a good girl, but I just can't.*

"Violet, you know that we don't talk to each other that way," Samantha said, taking the empty seat next to her. "Are you nervous about tomorrow?"

Violet took another bite of her sandwich, set it down, and nodded as she chewed.

"We're nervous about it, too," Samantha said, leaning down to make eye contact. "But we're hopeful. And just like we already talked about, we're not making any decisions on this trip."

Violet nodded, her skepticism preventing her from speaking.

"Marilyn, the woman that I've been talking to on the phone, is very excited to meet you tomorrow. I think you'll like her." Samantha started to unwrap her sandwich and looked over at her husband, who was still sitting on the bed. He rose and took the other seat at the desk that was serving as a makeshift dining table. Ian smiled at Samantha, hopeful that what she said was true.

Violet sat her sandwich down, using her very best manners. "What if they don't like me, Mom?"

"Then they're crazy, and we'll leave immediately. No questions asked." Samantha reached over and squeezed her daughter's arm. Violet accepted that answer, and she stared off at the wall while she finished her dinner.

Just after lunch the next day, the Durkins loaded their overnight bags, climbed into their car, and drove to Prader-Willi Homes of Oconomowoc. Violet tilted her head against the window. The trees seemed to fly by, mostly green but starting to show yellow and orange, letting Violet know that the warm fall wouldn't last forever. She liked being out in the country. The openness of the world reminded her of her grandparents' house, with no skyscrapers blocking the sun and no elevated train noisily chugging over her head. She looked at the lawns on the houses and imagined kids walking to school. Her mind was overloaded with how different city kids' lives were. This looked like the families that she saw on TV, the kids walking to school with their friends; Violet bet they were able to do things like go get milkshakes together. She'd never been able to do things like that—not that she had friends to do those things with anyway.

The large sign that proclaimed that they'd arrived at Oconomowoc Residential Programs broke Violet's thoughts.

Ian pulled the car around a corner and parked. Violet was shrinking against the door, and he closed his eyes for a moment, saying a silent prayer that everything he'd read and felt about Prader-Willi Homes of Oconomowoc was real. He glanced over at Samantha, who was perfecting her lipstick before getting out of the car. Despite the aging effect that the past six months had on them both, the only permanent mark they'd left on her, physically, were small crow's feet at the corners of her eyes. Her blonde bob looked exactly the same as it had ten years earlier when she was creeping up on her fifties. Ian knew that all three of them were equally nervous, and while Violet tried to hide and Samantha primped, Ian was a nervous talker. It took everything he had not to discuss the scenery and the weather, as he knew that it would only further boost Sam and Vi's anxiety.

Ian opened the door for Violet, offering his hand to her as she rose from the car and clasping her hand in his for reassurance. Samantha turned and smiled, taking

Violet's other hand. They walked across the parking lot, each enjoying the warmth of the other's hands, and Violet, for the first time in a long time, feeling like she had each of her parents beside her.

"You must be the Durkin family! Welcome!" A tall woman with a big smile stood behind a desk. Behind her were a shorter woman with cropped dark hair and a woman with long blond hair. "I'm Marilyn," the tall woman said. Turning to the shorter woman, she said, "This is Kelly, our house manager for the home that we'll be looking at today, and this is Lauren, the clinical coordinator who works with the people in that home. It's so nice to finally meet you all!"

Samantha dropped Violet's hand and walked over to Marilyn. Samantha extended her hand for a handshake, then quickly dropped her arm and embraced the woman. Violet was perplexed; her mother didn't hug anyone who wasn't family. She looked up at her father, whose eyes were filled with tears.

"It's wonderful to meet you all," Ian said.

"You must be Violet." Kelly extended her hand to the girl. "You're even prettier than your mom described."

Violet blushed and shook her hand, amazed that Kelly actually spoke to her. She wasn't used to people acknowledging her—they mostly only talked to her parents about her, as if she wasn't even in the room. "Thank you," Violet said quietly.

Lauren then extended her hand, and Violet blushed again. "We are very glad you came to visit today, Violet, and want to learn all about you while you're here."

Violet again quietly said, "Thank you," before stepping behind her father, attempting to hide.

"Well, shall we begin with a tour of one of our houses?" Marilyn asked as she walked over beside Ian. She smelled like honeysuckle, which was Violet's favorite scent.

"Do you use honeysuckle lotion?" Violet near-whispered, still behind her father.

"I do, Violet. Good nose." Marilyn smiled.

"It's my favorite," Violet said, taking a timid step out from behind her dad.

"Mine, too. I have some at my desk. Would you like some before we go see the home?"

Violet nodded, and Marilyn returned in just a moment with a familiar light pink bottle. She squirted a dollop of the thick cream into the palm of Violet's left hand and then tossed the bottle back onto her desk. Violet rubbed her hands together and pulled them close to her nose, smiling at the fragrance.

In the Durkins' car, Ian and Samantha sat in the front seat; Marilyn and Kelly sat in the back seat with Violet between them. Lauren said she would meet them all at the house and got into her own car. While Marilyn gave Ian directions, Kelly tried to strike up a conversation with Violet.

"So, Violet, how do you feel about your visit today?" Kelly asked, keeping her tone light and neutral.

Violet lowered her head, casting her eyes down to her lap.

"It's normal to be a little nervous. Everyone gets nervous with change," Kelly said. Violet looked up. "Does everyone that lives here have Prader-Willi?" Her innocent green eyes were wide with the question.

"Yes," Kelly said. "Everyone who lives with us has Prader-Willi Syndrome. Those are the only people we work with at PWHO. Our goal is to help you become as independent as possible."

Violet was skeptical. "What does that mean? What do you do?"

"We have a structured environment, much like what your parents do for you at home. We also have fun activities for the people who live with us, like Special Olympics sports and movie nights."

"Is a structured environment like a schedule?" Violet asked. "I need a schedule to feel good about things."

"It is. There are copies of the schedule posted in the house. I'll show it to you." Kelly looked right into Violet's eyes, and Violet thought she was telling the truth.

"What's on the schedule?" Violet asked.

"Well, we start the day with breakfast," Kelly replied. "Sometimes I come down to the table and talk to everyone. After breakfast, our people go to work. When they come home in the afternoon, everyone has time to get things done, such as laundry, housekeeping, or personal needs shopping. In the afternoon, we have sports, like I talked about, or we all go for a walk and do exercises, which is a big part of the program. Later, we try to do fun things, like have socials with other houses, go bowling, watch movies, or just relax."

Those things all sounded wonderful to Violet and a far cry from the life that she was leaving behind. She still wasn't sure that her life could be so full, and she was happy that her parents were with her today.

"Is there enough food here?" Violet asked, starting to look up at Kelly. Everything sounded okay so far.

"There is. Our residents get three meals and two snacks a day. We have kitchens in each home, and our staff prepares healthy food for everyone." Marilyn smiled at Violet.

"I always ask about food. My mind focuses on it, and I want to talk about it all the time. A lot of times, I get upset and do bad things." Violet's face was stoic, and although she was repeating things her psychiatrist had told her almost verbatim, she understood the meaning of what she was saying.

"I think asking about food is important, and it's a great question, Violet," Kelly said. "We understand how hard it is to stop thinking and talking about food. Here at PWHO, we all eat together and make smart food choices that will help us become healthy. You will have a copy of our schedule, which will include our meal times every day so that you can see when we'll be eating. More importantly, we have a lot of fun away from our dinner table."

Violet finally seemed satisfied, and Samantha felt relief wash warm over her body. Violet was talking with people who actually understood her. In the few minutes that Violet had interacted with Marilyn and Kelly, she had relaxed a little. These women were talking to her, showing interest in her concerns. Samantha was thrilled.

Following Marilyn's directions, Ian pulled into the driveway of the first home. The white brick house spread across the lot, with a roomy wraparound porch and three rocking chairs swaying in the early afternoon breeze. Ian sighed inwardly, letting go of the fear that it would look like the last place. Lauren pulled up and joined them just as they walked to the front door. She explained, "Usually the clinical coordinators don't have an office in the home, but I'm lucky because I get to have one in this house." She smiled at Violet.

"The residents and staff are at work right now, but we can look around the house," Marilyn said with a smile.

Violet paused. "At *work?*" she asked her mother.

"Yes, Vi. Remember that we talked about the residents here having jobs?" Samantha reminded her daughter. "Marilyn and Kelly mentioned it, too."

Kelly smiled. "This is all a lot to take in," she said to the family.

Violet's enthusiasm was palpable. "But they're all like me," she said, making a statement more than asking a question. She looked between the adults. "They're all like me, and they have real *jobs?*"

Kelly laughed and nodded. "That's right, Violet. I'm happy to see you're excited about that."

They all walked into the living room, which was set up with a couch and two armchairs in front of a television on a hutch. The house smelled like carpet freshener and lemon wipes. *Very homey*, thought Violet, as she followed the group through the room. They walked into the kitchen, where brown wooden cabinets were fitted with small metallic holes where a key would enter, and Violet nodded, knowing this was what she needed. In the dining room, a large wooden table was set up, flanked by brick walls and a fireplace.

"It's pretty here," Violet said, breaking the quiet conversation between Marilyn, Lauren, and her parents. While Samantha and Ian were impressed with the home, they were trying to keep their opinions to themselves until Violet expressed hers.

"It is," Samantha agreed. "Vi, would you mind sitting with Kelly for a few minutes? Marilyn, Dad, and I going to go back to Lauren's office for a bit."

Violet looked at both of her parents. "Are you going to talk about me?" Her hands balled into fists, anxiety rising. She hated when anyone talked about her.

"Only boring stuff," Ian said, rubbing Violet's arm. "You'd have more fun here with Kelly than with us."

"Okay," Violet agreed reluctantly. "Will you come right back?"

"Of course. We'll be back before you even realize we're gone," Samantha said, as Lauren led them to the other room.

"Have a seat, Violet." Kelly pointed to the living room couch. "Would you like a glass of water?"

Violet looked around. "Do you have Diet Coke?"

"No. Just water." Kelly smiled.

Violet nodded and Kelly disappeared into the kitchen, where Violet heard a jingle of keys. In just a moment, she came back with two bottles of cold water. She opened them both and handed one to Violet before taking a seat next to her on the couch.

"Do you have kids?" Violet asked, looking over at the plain wedding band on Kelly's left hand.

"I do," Kelly smiled. "Two of them. They're still little."

"What are their names?" Violet asked, turning her body towards Kelly in conversation.

"Benjamin and Lilly. They're six and two."

"Are they smart? Do they have Prader-Willi?" Violet asked, leaning back into the couch.

"Those are two separate questions that have nothing to do with each other. But, yes, I think they're smart; and no, they don't have Prader-Willi," Kelly responded.

"I'm smart, too. I walked with my high school class in May. I was supposed to go back to school this fall, but

I didn't. I was bad. Mitchell got mad at my party," Violet said, looking at Kelly as if she'd confided something major in her.

"I see, Violet. Did that make you mad?" Kelly asked.

"No. It made me sad. Mitchell was in college, and he came back. He wasn't making good choices, and then he left. Sometimes I'm bad, too," Violet said.

Kelly opened her mouth to respond, but a key in the door indicated that the residents had come back from work. The seven people who walked in the door saw her and ran right over.

"Hi, what's your name?" A girl a few years older than Violet extended her hand.

"Violet," she quietly responded.

The girl sat down next to Violet. She flipped her blonde hair over her shoulder and leaned toward her. "I'm Stephanie. Are you coming to live with us? Do you have Prader-Willi?"

"Yeah. Do you?" Violet asked.

"Yep. I work in a factory. I check packages before they are mailed out. I love my job, but today I got mad. Do you get mad sometimes?" Stephanie crinkled her freckled nose and squinted at Violet behind her thick glasses.

"Sometimes I get mad," Violet responded, amazed at the quick connection they were forming.

"Are you going to live here? I don't have a roommate anymore, so if you live here, you'll room with me," Stephanie said. "You would be happy here, Violet. Do you like to watch TV? I do. We'll be best friends."

"I have never had a best friend before," Violet said, her heart bursting at the offer.

Stephanie reached over and hugged her. "You do now."

Kelly cleared her throat. "Violet, your parents are in the driveway."

"But I want to talk to Stephanie," Violet protested.

"Yes, and there will be plenty of time to talk later. Right now we need to get you into the car so that you can talk to them."

"Okay," Violet reluctantly agreed. "Stephanie, I promise that I'll be your roommate—that we'll talk again as soon as we can."

"That's wonderful!" Stephanie exclaimed and smiled at Violet as Kelly led her to the door.

Violet climbed into the backseat of her parents' car. She pulled herself to the center and leaned in between the seats.

"I want to go home to get my stuff," Violet announced. "I have a best friend who will be my roommate here. Her name is Stephanie, and we're going to watch TV together. I need to be back soon."

"First things first, Violet," Ian said through a whoosh of relief. "We need to have some conversations about the way this is going to work. Did you really love it here? Do you think you could be happy?"

"I do!" Violet exclaimed, happier than she'd sounded in a long time.

. . .

Three months later, Ian and Samantha were in the backyard, working in the garden. Lukas had come home for a week before he began his fall semester, and he was inside with Violet, teaching her to play checkers. Ian pulled his head up from the dirt when he heard his cell phone ring. It was Mrs. Posey. Ian took a deep breath, called out to Samantha, and picked it up with a soil-caked hand.

"Hello?" Ian answered.

"Is Samantha home?" Mrs. Posey asked, her voice bubbling with vigor.

"Yeah, I'll put you on speaker," Ian said, pushing the button on his phone.

"Hello, Mrs. Posey," Samantha said.

"According to the school district, Violet is now officially funded as a resident at PWHO in Wisconsin!"

"Really?" Ian was thrilled by the news. He didn't have any doubt in Mrs. Posey but was surprised at how quickly she'd pushed everything through.

"We'll get Violet to PWHO, since that's where you want her. You made a great case. You both went above and beyond in providing me with all the necessary documentation. I know this was a lot of hard work for your family, but you've done it! Violet's funding should be approved in about two weeks." The Durkins could hear Mrs. Posey smiling through the phone. "We will send a formal referral packet to Marilyn, so we need you to sign a release. I'll get in touch with Marilyn to confirm our intent to place Violet there. Then she'll send you a pre-admission packet. You'll have to complete parts of this, and we'll need to do a joint IEP phone meeting with them before we can set a date."

"Thank you," Samantha said, her voice full of emotion. "Thank you for everything."

Ian stumbled to a patio chair, where he sat in stunned silence. The dark cloud of wondering what was next had cleared. He hadn't even realized how much the waiting game was affecting him, but now that it was finished, he felt the way he did when he was finally done with medical school: he'd been looking forward to it for so long that once he had it, he wasn't sure what to do with it.

CHAPTER 13

Beep, beep, beep. Violet's alarm buzzed on her nightstand. She rubbed her eyes and let them slowly adjust to the dark room. Even though she'd lived in Wisconsin for almost two weeks, she was still sometimes unsure where she was when awake. She yawned and stretched, sitting up in bed to put on her slippers. Tuesday mornings were her scheduled days to shower, so she shuffled down the hall to the bathroom to begin her morning routine.

After her shower, Violet went downstairs to weigh in and to get her medications before taking her seat at the table. The schedule called for breakfast at exactly seven-thirty in the morning. She was ready for her food, and two of her housemates—her new friends, Dane and Patrick—sat on either side of her. Growing up with brothers, she was used to living with boys, but sometimes Dane and Patrick were really annoying.

At the head of the table, Kelly modeled clasping her hands in front of her, and all of the residents quieted and did the same. Suzanne, the staff member that morning, brought out each individual's breakfast; everyone's hands remained folded until the whole table had been served. The staff stressed that was just good manners. Suzanne put cereal, milk, and grapes in front of Violet.

The primary goal of the first few weeks was to get her comfortable, and it was working well so far.

Violet looked over as Suzanne gave Patrick cereal, milk, and grapes, too. Everyone got the same meals but different portions. They all needed different amounts to be healthy; at least that was what Violet had been told. When the portions that seemed meager to Violet were placed before her, she always felt a pang of desire for more. Kelly said that the nutritionist had worked with everyone to determine how much food each person needed. Even if she still never felt full, Violet felt reassured to know when her next meal was coming.

"Good morning, everyone," Kelly started. "How is everyone feeling today?"

The residents nodded, and a few mumbled, "Good."

"Today, I want to share a story with you all about a sad skunk." On some days, Kelly liked to start the day with a story. "He didn't have any friends because he smelled. Nobody wanted to be around him, because he would spray. So the sad skunk was lonely, and he happened to be walking along the trail one day and saw a pair of poor bunnies that were so frightened because there was a fox there wanting to eat them. The skunk ran up to the scene, stuck his butt to the fox, and sprayed his stink all over. The fox was horrified and ran away. The bunnies were so happy the skunk saved them that they didn't mind how he smelled. He was their best friend in the world, and the sad skunk wasn't sad anymore."[1]

The room was silent for a full minute, each resident ruminating over the story. Violet knew that Kelly's stories

---

1   Davis, Nancy, Ph.D. *Once Upon a Time: Therapeutic Stories that Teach and Heal.* Burke, VA: Nancy Davis, Ph.D. 2006.

always had a point bigger than the story, and she let this one roll through her mind so that she could find the meaning.

"So, everyone, that was a pretty neat story, huh?" Kelly smiled at the table. "Violet, what do you think about that?"

Violet thought for a minute before answering. "I think the story is kind of like having Prader-Willi. Before I came to live here, I had trouble making friends, because nobody liked me. I was like the skunk. I can't save anybody, but now that I'm here with my friends, life is a lot happier."

"That's a very interesting thought, Violet. What do the rest of you think?" Kelly asked.

"I agree with what Violet said," said Gwen thoughtfully. "I mean, so many people look at us and only see we have a syndrome. Everyone thinks PW is a disability and that we can't do things. But I think it also comes with lots of good things. While we can't always control our temper or our appetite, my dad always says that he's never met anyone as determined as I am. He says that instead of calling me stubborn! We can all do a lot of things if we're given a chance, if someone will teach us, and understand that sometimes it just takes us longer. We've all become good friends here, too; and that's something good, right? A lot of things are good."

"That is a great insight," Kelly said, smiling at Gwen's revelation. "Does anyone else want to say anything?" She looked around, and when no one raised their hand or said anything, she continued, "Well, friends, I'll let you all finish your breakfast. We're leaving for work in exactly twenty minutes."

. . .

The clock read 11:50, and Violet had just finished her last package before lunch. She took great pride in her work at the local factory, checking to ensure that each piece of the package was there so that when the people received their stuff, they would be happy. She loved thinking that her job was important, not only to the company for which she worked, but also to the people who would find everything complete in their boxes. Violet heard Suzanne call out that it was time to wash hands and eat in the cafeteria. She followed her co-workers toward the sinks and then to the special room the factory set up so that residents from PWHO could eat their lunches together.

Violet sat down at one of the long rectangular tables, next to Gwen. Suzanne passed out the lunches. Everyone had their own insulated lunch box that they had picked out themselves. Violet dumped the contents of her box and was pleased to find a turkey sandwich on thin bread with mustard and veggies, a baggie of baby carrots, apple slices, and skim milk. Her excitement took over, and she ripped the saran wrap from the sandwich and bit off nearly half of it.

"Slow down, Violet. I don't want you to choke," Gwen said, looking over to Violet with a smile.

Violet nodded, unable to speak. She swallowed carefully and smiled back at Gwen. "Okay. You're right. I was hurrying. You don't hurry. Did you learn that here? How long have you lived here?"

"I've been here for almost twenty years," Gwen said. "I lived by myself for a lot of years before I was able to be here. I weighed over three hundred pounds, but I've been able to get healthy living here."

"That's good. I hope that I can be healthy, too," Violet said, smiling at her friend.

"You will, Violet." Gwen stopped short. She looked across the table at Dane, who was laughing with Patrick.

"What is it, Dane?" Gwen yelled across the table. "Do you see something funny?"

"No. What are you talking about?" Dane asked, his face confused.

Gwen shoved her chair back, standing up. "Why do you have to be so nasty all the time? No one asked you what you thought. Violet and I were having a private conversation, Dane! You know better than to listen to girls' private talk!"

Dane stood up and yelled back at Gwen. Violet couldn't understand what he was saying, but he was just as mad.

Violet didn't like when people yelled, and she blocked out the noise around her. She looked down, trying to avoid the confrontation around her, when she was suddenly distracted by Gwen's lunch. The apple slices were sitting, unsupervised, across Gwen's plastic bag. Violet was still chewing her last apple slice and didn't think Gwen would notice if she just took one of hers. Violet's stomach roared in anticipation of the literal forbidden fruit. The gurgling rose up into her throat as that white noise filled her mind, telling her to get food, to eat, and Violet could almost feel the cool, slippery texture on her fingers when Suzanne suddenly put her hand on Violet's shoulder.

"Violet. What are you doing?" Suzanne asked.

"Nothing!" Violet sat straight up, the anticipation turning into cold fear in her veins. She had been making such good choices and didn't want to ruin that with one mistake.

"Violet, we each have our own lunches so that we can

all be healthy. Those apples are Gwen's," Suzanne said, making eye contact.

Violet looked down at her hands. "I know. I'm sorry."

"It's okay, Violet. You need to keep working on that, though." Suzanne patted Violet on her shoulder as she rose to resume her post against the wall. Another staff member was working to calm Gwen.

"I will keep trying. I'm sorry, Suzanne," Violet muttered, embarrassed that she'd almost stolen from her friend.

"It's okay, Vi," Suzanne said.

Violet was looking forward to her individual talk with Lauren—who had set up special times to meet with her right after she moved in—and counted the last few minutes of work until she could return home. When Violet got home, she washed her face and hands and then went to Lauren's office, settling on the love seat across from the swivel chair where Lauren always sat during her chats with the residents. Violet reached over and picked up a slinky that Lauren kept on the table between them. She moved it up and down, feeling each spring add weight to the alternating hand.

"So, you've been here for two weeks now, Violet. How are you settling in?" Lauren asked.

Violet thought about the question before responding. "I like it here. I get to be a grown up."

"What does that mean to you, Violet?" Lauren asked, leaning forward.

"I get to go to work every morning. I live with my friends, just like a grown up does," Violet responded matter-of-factly.

"Yes. You do. Tell me more about how you feel about that," Lauren said.

"I'm really happy. At home, my brothers looked out for me and helped me try out new things. I did everything that they did, played with them, and went to school. I didn't get to go to college like my brothers did. I always knew that I was different from them, but when they were gone, I felt sad. I had to stay home, while they got to move away. My parents wanted to keep me at home, and no one was happy. But now, I can be a grown up like them. It's easier to make good choices when I feel like I am important," Violet said.

"You are important, Violet," Lauren said. "Did you feel like you weren't important when you were at home?"

"I know I'm important to my parents. I know they love me. They tell me those things all the time. But, here, I'm important to other people, too. My job is important. If I don't go to work, the factory can't get my job done without me. My friends are important. They love me," Violet responded.

"I'm so glad to hear that you're doing so well. What are you looking forward to?"

"I want to learn how to make better choices. I want to turn off the voice that tells me I'm hungry," Violet said, in confessional tone.

"We can certainly work on that, Violet, but we have to take it in steps. That drive, or the voice as you call it, might not ever go away. What we're going to work toward right now is trying to help you ignore those voices by doing other, different things and by making you feel safer. The things that are hard for you to control will get better when you feel safer."

Violet nodded. She just wanted to feel safe.

Lauren smiled. "That's good, Violet. Thank you so

much for talking to me today. Now, why don't we to get ready for our walk?"

...

After dinner, Violet went into the bathroom to do her nightly hygiene before she went to sleep. She washed her face and looked up at herself in the mirror, and for a moment, she pretended she was beautiful. Her almond-shaped eyes shifted farther apart from each other, growing wider, with long lashes. She reached to the top of her scalp to smooth the long, curly blonde hair that she imagined but was disappointed to find that her head was still covered with her flat, frizzy, auburn hair. Why couldn't she have just one of the things that she wanted in life? Prader-Willi Syndrome had robbed her of her will; why did it also have to give her such a funky appearance? She could never be pictured on the cover of any of the fashion magazines that Stephanie read. Before she knew what she was doing, her hands reached her hairline and twined chunks of flat, brown hair around her fingers. Furiously, she pulled her hair, the anger in her veins only relieved with the pain on her scalp. Blood trickled down her forehead, and it just made her angrier.

The bathroom door opened, and Suzanne stuck her head around the door. "Violet, you've been in here for a while, I wanted to check on you—" She stopped when she saw the blood on Violet's face. "Oh, sweetie. What are you doing?"

Violet turned around to face her, rubbing her forehead with her hands. "Nothing," she said dully.

"Oh, sweetie. Let's go get you cleaned up and see if you can talk to Lauren." After Suzanne got Violet cleaned up, she guided her down the hallway and into Lauren's office.

Lauren was just getting ready to leave for the day, but when she saw the blood and bald spot on Violet, she dropped her bag and sat down.

"I pulled out my hair," Violet said, just above a whisper.

"I see that. What's going on?" Lauren sat Violet down on the love seat and took a seat beside her. She nodded to let Suzanne know she had this situation under control, and Suzanne walked back into the other room.

"I just want to be pretty. I want to be popular and have a boyfriend. I just want to have fun," Violet said.

"Well, earlier today, when we talked, you said you were happy," Lauren reminded her gently, concerned.

"I am happy—but I'm only as happy as Violet can be. I'm not as happy as a pretty girl can be. I'm not as happy as anyone without Prader-Willi can be." Violet's eyes filled with tears.

"We have to think of something that will make you feel better without hurting yourself. Do you have any ideas?" Lauren asked.

Violet shrugged. "A hair cut?"

"Sure. What were you thinking?"

"My brothers watched a weird movie one time. The girl was really pretty, with a really short haircut. A pixie cut, I guess. I don't remember what the movie was called, but she was blonde and thin. She was scared a lot. No one knew that I watched it—I snuck around to see it," Violet confided. "Anyway, I think that if my hair was cut like hers, I'd feel better. She was so pretty."

"Hmm . . ." Lauren said. "*Rosemary's Baby?* Was that the movie?"

"Yes!" Violet exclaimed, looking at Lauren in awe for

guessing it right away.

Lauren smiled. "I think you could look lovely with Mia Farrow's haircut, and if it's short, you won't be able to pull it out as easily. If we get you that haircut, do you promise to try to talk to someone the next time you feel like hurting yourself?" Lauren asked, looking Violet in the eye.

"Really? I can go to the salon and get my hair done, just like my mom does?" Violet was thrilled.

"You certainly may. I'll talk it over with the staff tomorrow, then check with your Mom to make sure it's okay, and we'll make an appointment. Would that make you feel better?" Lauren asked.

Violet's whole body tingled with excitement. "Yes!"

CHAPTER 14

After living at PWHO for six months, Violet had lost an as-tonishing sixty pounds and fallen into her routine nicely. She got up on a Tuesday morning to perform her morning hygiene, and when she lowered her pajama pants and underwear to use the bathroom, she was shocked to find them spotted with blood. *I'm dying,* she thought. *Something is really wrong with me, and I'm going to die.* Anxiety set in, making Violet's blood run cold, and she involuntarily fell from the toilet to her knees, her body wracked with sobs.

"Violet, what is it?" Kelly came rushing into the bath-room to find Violet on all fours. She had been getting prepared for the home's morning session when she'd heard a crash from the bathroom followed by Violet's cries. "What's wrong?" She bent down next to Violet, who couldn't speak through her tears and screams but pointed to the underwear that were now around her knees.

"Violet, I can't see any . . ." Kelly trailed off. She saw the dark blood contrasting with the white cotton cloth and knew that she and Violet had to have a talk.

After calming Violet, explaining to her that she wasn't dying and helping her maneuver the additional steps in her hygiene routine, Kelly left to excuse Violet from work that morning. Then she called Lauren to let her know what had happened, and finally she called Samantha.

Although Samantha got calls from Kelly regularly, they were usually in the evening, and she was concerned that something was wrong with her daughter.

"Kelly, is Violet okay?" she asked, her focus completely on the phone call.

"She's fine, Sam. Well, she's a little freaked out, but she's a woman," Kelly said, smiling.

"Wait, what?" Samantha asked. "Are you saying . . ."

"I am. Violet started to menstruate this morning. She didn't know anything, so I gave her a basic overview. I didn't want to cross any boundaries with you, so it would be great if you could give her a call this evening. I've already talked to Lauren about it, so she is aware. Violet's in her bed now. I excused her from work for the morning."

"Of course, I'll call her. I never talked to her about her body because I never thought we would have to. She started puberty at twelve, but the only thing I had to do then was buy her a small bra and explain that her body was changing." Samantha's voice was filled with tearful wonder. "Our doctors told us that if it ever happened, it would be infrequent and would probably escape notice, and by the time she turned sixteen and nothing happened at all, I just kind of gave up on it. She asked me what a tampon was—I guess she'd heard girls talk about them at school—and I explained it to her, but she didn't have any interest, so I didn't push the talk."

"Until recently, your doctor was absolutely right," Kelly said. "In fact, I believe that PWHO was the first provider to report that some of their female clients had started menstruating. At least to our knowledge, it had never been reported and it wasn't studied. Violet has lost a considerable amount of weight in the past six months. According to her medical records, this is the thinnest that she's ever been. Isn't that right?" Kelly asked.

A light bulb went off in Samantha's mind. "It is. You're right. Do you think that her weight prevented her from reaching sexual maturity?"

"There is certainly a link between weight and one's reproductive organs," Kelly said. "In PWHO's history, we've found that as women with Prader-Willi maintain a healthier weight and lifestyle, they may experience some physical changes and maybe hormonal functioning, one of which is the onset of menses. It doesn't always happen, but it does with a significant number. Now, obviously, since this is Violet's first cycle, we can't say what hers will look like. We've found that although some women's come on a schedule, mostly the cycles are light and sporadic, and they come and go," Kelly said.

Samantha's head was spinning with all this new information. "I'll call her this afternoon. Could we do it so that we're all together on a conference call? I'd feel better knowing that she has you with her, Kelly."

"Sure. Lauren and I can both be on the call. Could we do five p.m.? If that doesn't work for Lauren, I'll let you know, but I think she will make it work," Kelly said, looking at her calendar.

"Perfect. Thank you." Samantha hung up the phone. She couldn't believe the changes in her daughter, physically, emotionally, and mentally since she'd moved to Wisconsin. Violet held her head high every time Samantha and Ian saw her, speaking with a confidence that reassured them that she was, finally, living up to her full potential.

...

Violet pulled out her day planner after work. It was more a diary than a calendar, really. In the nine months that Violet had lived at PWHO, she found that she had as much to keep up with as any other adult. She kept all of her important dates and Special Olympics basketball practices, and she'd kept track of her cycles for the past three months. Violet looked at the calendar before her and smiled. Even though she was done with work, she still had a big day ahead of her. She'd spent the previous weekend at home, and while she loved seeing her family, she was always relieved to get back to her own life in Wisconsin. After work, she wanted to talk to Lauren, and then she had practice with her Special Olympics basketball team.

She walked down the hall to Lauren's office, where her clinical coordinator was waiting for her.

"Hey Vi." Lauren smiled as she gave her a hug.

"Hey, Lore," Violet laughed. No one outside of her family had ever called her Vi, and while she loved that Lauren did, she wanted to give her a one-syllable nickname, too.

Violet sat on the love seat while Lauren took her place in the swivel chair. "So, you were able to go home last weekend. How was that?" Lauren asked, opening a steno pad and getting a pen ready to take notes.

"It was good," Violet said. "I started my period while I was there. It was weird to tell my mom that I needed to buy pads. I buy them during my personal needs shopping trip and always have enough so that I never have to tell anyone when I need them. Mom was cool about it, though. She just took me to the drug store and we got some."

"That's great, Violet. Our relationship with our parents changes when we become adults, and it can be tricky trying to figure out how we can do things with them. Were you embarrassed?" Lauren asked.

"Yes, but it was okay because it was just Mom and me. It was our girl time," Violet said, before looking at her feet.

Lauren could see that Violet wanted to say something else—something more than an uncomfortable request for a box of pads from the store. "Violet, you don't sound very good." Lauren leaned in. "Is something else bothering you?"

"When we went to buy pads at the drug store, Mom bought me a candy bar. It wasn't meal or snack time, and she just let me eat the whole thing. She told me that if I had my period, chocolate would make me feel better. I know that when I'm here, you and I talk about my mind and how it always tells me that I'm hungry and that no food will ever make me feel better. That weekend, we didn't totally keep to our schedule. Mom said we were celebrating. Mom even made me a second plate once. I didn't even ask! It was very different than here—very different than when I lived at home before." Violet had been staring down at her hands the whole time she'd spoken, but she finally met Lauren's gaze. "I know I'm not supposed to tattle, but you asked me what was wrong, and that's it."

"Violet, you're not tattling when you tell me how you feel," Lauren reassured her. "Did you not feel safe?"

"I felt safe, but I'm not supposed to have extra. That confused me. I gained six pounds in three days," Violet said. "I guess gaining weight is not safe for me. My family wasn't thinking about me becoming healthy, and that's what I think about now that I live here."

"I see. Violet, you've lost seventy pounds in the last eight months and kept it off for a month now. That's a great way to become healthy. Gaining weight back is not healthy, though," Lauren said.

"I just don't know what to do," Violet said. "I had so much fun with my parents, but I'm afraid that I won't be able to see them anymore if I go off my diet."

"What would make you feel safe, Violet?" Lauren asked. "What do you think was missing that can be changed?"

Violet sat thoughtfully for a moment. "Well, it was the diet and the schedule. But I don't have basketball and work and walks at home, so I don't know how the schedule would work."

"What if we made the suggestion that you keep your meal schedule the same, even if the rest of the schedule is different?" Lauren suggested. "How could we make that happen when you're at home?"

"I could give my parents a copy of our weekend schedule before I go home the next time. I could ask them to please use that. Do you think that would sound bossy?" Violet asked, proving to Lauren that she had grown as a person—that she was truly concerned with her parents' feelings and how she was perceived.

"I don't think it will sound bossy at all. I have an idea. Let's call your parents and talk to them about that," Lauren said, smiling.

"No! I will hurt their feelings if I tell them I don't feel safe at home!" Violet drew back into herself on the couch.

"You know what, Violet? I bet you don't. You're a woman

now. You had to tell your mom that you needed pads this trip, which was something different. You dealt with that well, and I'm sure that you'll be able to handle this well, too. I bet they will be happy to talk to you about it, like adults talk about things." Lauren smiled at Violet again. She'd come so far in the past eight months, but she was still learning.

Violet wiped her sweaty palms on her jeans. She knew that she could talk to her parents about her fear, but she was scared that she would make them unhappy and they wouldn't take her home for visits anymore. Things had been so rough when she left, and she was relieved to see a look of joy in her father's eyes when he saw her on the weekends, instead of the look of dread that he'd carried with him for months before that.

"I'm going to dial them on speaker phone," Lauren said. "I told them that we might be calling this afternoon, so they're expecting a call."

Violet just nodded nervously.

"Hello?" Samantha's voice answered, and Violet felt a pang of guilt at the conversation she was about to have with them. Her mother sounded so happy, and Violet didn't ever want to take that happiness away from her again.

"Hi, Mom," Violet said quietly.

"Hey, Vi, how are you, sweetie?" Samantha's voice warmed even more when she heard her daughter.

"I'm good, Mom," Violet mumbled and then took a deep breath. When adults had a problem, they talked about it, and she was an adult. She could do this. "Mom, I—"

"Hold on just a minute. Your dad is picking up the other phone," Samantha said.

"Hey, angel," Ian's voice came through clearly.

"Hey, Daddy," Violet replied, smiling herself now.

"I'm here, too, everyone," Lauren said, inserting herself in the conversation at just the right moment.

"Well, what's going on, ladies?" Ian asked.

"Violet and I have been talking about her home visit, and we wanted to include you both on this conversation," Lauren said.

"Sure," Samantha replied.

"When Violet got back to PWHO, she had gained six pounds over the weekend," Lauren said, broaching the conversation with a fact that was indisputable by all parties.

Samantha and Ian were quiet. After a moment, Lauren continued, "She and I were talking about why that happened, and we think we've come to a solution. Violet, would you tell your parents what we talked about?"

Violet nodded, looking at Lauren as she spoke. "When I lived at home with you, we had our days planned out. Now that I live at PWHO, we have our days planned out even more. When I came home last weekend, we didn't have our days planned."

"Oh, sweetie," Ian said.

"Violet told me that the lack of schedule or routine can make her feel unsafe. Right, Violet?" Lauren asked, looking back at the girl.

Violet nodded.

"Vi, your parents can't hear you nodding," Lauren reminded her.

"Yes," Violet said. "I'm sorry, Mom and Dad."

"We're the ones who should apologize, Violet." Samantha's voice was soft. "We've been so excited to hang out with you, to be your *parents*, that we decided to bend the rules when you got here and indulge you a little. We made bad choices, and we never meant to make you feel unsafe. We're so sorry, Vi."

Violet was surprised at her mother's reaction. She didn't expect that talking about these things would be so easy, but in that moment, she realized how everyone had changed since she'd moved to PWHO. "It's okay, Mom," she said. "Before I come home next time, I'll send you a copy of my schedule."

"Of course, Violet," Ian said. "We would be more than happy to adjust ourselves back to your school schedule, instead of trying to keep a loose version of what we did a year ago. We can accept that what you're doing now is working well for you, and we're sorry that we didn't keep things that way before."

Violet was smiling from ear to ear. She was thrilled with the way that the conversation had gone, but more importantly, she felt confident that she could use her words to make her point. She didn't have to melt down when she had a problem.

"Let's plan on chatting again in a few weeks, before Violet goes back home," Lauren said, wrapping up the call. She wanted to end this conversation on a good note so that Violet left the call feeling positive.

"We love you, Violet," Samantha said.

"I love you too," Violet said. "Goodbye."

"How did you feel about that?" Lauren asked after she pushed the end button.

"I feel good. Really good," Violet said, smiling broadly.

"Did you think you could do that? That it would be so easy?" Lauren smiled. "I knew that you could."

"No. But, I'm glad I did it. My parents know that I'm a grown up, too. I can tell them what's going on with me, and they will understand or at least try to. I think it's hard for people who don't have Prader-Willi to think about these things," Violet said.

"I think that's very true, Violet. Now—" Lauren stood up with a grin. "You need to get ready to be on the basketball court in fifteen minutes!"

Violet rose for a hug before walking back to her room to put on her new gym shoes.

CHAPTER 15

"Did you already use the blue bag?" Samantha called out to Ian. They were packing their things for a long weekend with Violet in Wisconsin. The week before had been her twentieth birthday, but she'd insisted that her parents wait to come the following weekend to watch her play in the Special Olympics basketball tournament that had been set up. Lukas had come into town for a long weekend and was going to ride up with them and then fly out of Madison back to California.

"I don't think so," Ian called back absently from the hallway. "I think it's in the back of the closet still. I've only packed my Dopp kit."

Samantha rolled her eyes. Of course, Ian hadn't packed anything yet. He always waited until the last minute. She could hear her husband making his way to the bedroom and was ready to lay into him, but when she looked up, she saw that he was holding a letter in which he was engrossed.

"What is it?" Samantha walked over to her husband.

"The school district. Her twentieth birthday. It snuck up on us so soon . . ." Ian trailed off and handed the letter to his wife. She looked down to read it.

Dear Dr. and Mrs. Durkin:

This letter is to inform you that Violet Julianne Durkin will no longer be eligible for continued funding for services at Prader-Willi Homes of Oconomowoc as of her twenty-first birthday, one calendar year from now.

We, the school district, are cooperating with the state in a transition to adult services, and we suggest that, as Violet's guardian, you start the process of initiating contact with a state intake worker to process her application for eligibility. If we can help in any way in this process, please don't hesitate to let me know.

Serving Violet has been our pleasure.

Sincerely,
Mrs. Elizabeth Posey

"What the hell?" Samantha said out loud. "I mean, I knew this was coming, but . . ." She sat down on the bed weakly. Ian joined her, putting his hand on the back of her neck.

"Well, we're already heading to Oconomowoc. I bet Marilyn has seen this before. We'll talk to her about it this weekend," Ian said, softly. "Let's just get to Vi. We can't let her know that anything is wrong. Nothing at all." Ian's eyes were comforting but serious.

Samantha sighed heavily. "You're right. If the universe is indeed a fair place, Violet will be able to stay where she is happy and loved." She was saying this as much to hear it out loud herself as to reassure Ian.

Samantha and Ian pulled into PWHO's offices and

sent Lukas to Violet's home to visit with her. Marilyn stood and greeted them with a big hug.

"How are you?" she exclaimed, her soft curls bouncing.

"We got this letter in the mail today," Ian said, exchanging no pleasantries and instead somberly placing the envelope into Marilyn's hand.

Marilyn opened the letter and glanced it over. "I see," she said. "We knew this would eventually happen, but it seems to have come so fast. This letter initiates the need to put the adult system process in motion."

"What does that mean?" Samantha asked.

"Violet just turned twenty, so her school district funding is expected to end in a year," Marilyn explained. "I was actually going to talk with you this week, but it seems that your vice principal knows her stuff. This letter verifies that the education system has met its responsibility and will be dropping out when Violet turns twenty-one, so Mrs. Posey is giving us notice, and it's time to get to work on this. At age twenty-one, Violet's care needs are the responsibility of the adult system at the state level. She will now require adult funding through the state to stay at PWHO."

"We knew this was going to happen, but what are we in for, Marilyn?" Ian asked, furrowing his brow.

"Well, you have this letter already, and you'll need to collect letters from everyone who has worked with Violet previously and here at PWHO. The process now is to file an application with the state for funding eligibility and build a case that will hopefully result in their allowing her to stay at PWHO for continued placement. The state systems are different. The first thing you need to do is start working with a social worker, like you did before

Violet came here. It is possible you will need support from advocates and maybe even an attorney." Marilyn chose her words carefully. She didn't want to frighten Samantha and Ian, but she wanted them to be prepared for the potential battle that could lay before them.

"Wait," Samantha interjected. "Are they going to try to put Violet back in a place like she was the first time?"

"The state does like to utilize in-state facilities as a first option," Marilyn replied. "You've been down that road before. We may be able to help connect you with resources in your state that have experience in this area, and we will help you as much as we can. You may also want to contact Mrs. Posey to see if she has any recommendations for who might be able to help."

Ian said, "I'll start making phone calls on Monday. Sam, can you contact a new state social worker? We'll get requests in for all the letters that we need from PWHO this weekend. It looks like we have to start all over."

Marilyn smiled and patted Ian on the arm. "This isn't easy, but you've both already fought so hard for Violet's life. It takes tough people to parent a child with Prader-Willi as well as you have with Violet."

Sunday night, the Durkins were exhausted and fell into bed as soon as they got home. "You going to call tomorrow?" Ian asked, his voice betraying that he wasn't anywhere near sleep, despite having the covers pulled up.

"I will. My morning is pretty clear, since I anticipated being tired after the weekend," Samantha said. She rolled over to face her husband. "I feel like we're starting all over, too, but I feel a little better about everything after talking with Marilyn. At least we'll get some support and guidance to resources that might help us through it this time. And Mrs. Posey has always worked so hard on Violet's behalf."

Ian wrapped his arms around his wife's waist—her middle that had carried all three of their babies when they weren't big enough to make it in the world without her. He owed her three lives, but with her unrelenting spirit for Violet's care, he felt like he owed her at least one more. He knew that she brought a unique strength to their marriage. He'd felt that strength in her the first time he laid eyes on her. His best friend from high school was marrying her best friend from college, and they'd both served as honor attendants in the wedding. At the rehearsal dinner, she glowed in a pink shift dress, her then long blonde hair falling in waves down her back— but she wasn't having a glass of champagne with the other bridesmaids. She was engrossed in serious conversation with the wedding planner, pointing to the layout of the reception hall, her scotch and rocks swaying in her free hand. Her carefully plucked eyebrows rose and fell with her words, and she was clearly making her point, not by bullying but by convincing the planner that there was a more efficient way.

"That's Samantha," said Jimmy, the groom, who snuck up behind Ian and caught him admiring her. "She's Veronica's maid of honor. They were roommates their freshman year of college. She's beautiful, but she's intense, man."

"What's her story?" Ian was interested and wasn't shy about letting his lifelong friend know. The two men had grown up in the same suburb, and while Jimmy had gone to Northwestern with Veronica, Ian had gone off to stake new claims after high school at Purdue. He was back in the city now, in his second year of medical school.

"She's at Harvard Business School. Definitely more than just a body," Jimmy said devilishly.

"Dude. You're getting married to her best friend tomorrow," Ian told his buddy jokingly.

"Don't get me wrong. I can admire, but Sam is definitely too much for me. She's been too much for a lot of guys, if I'm remembering our undergraduate days properly." Jimmy laughed. "I'd love to make an introduction, though. Just don't take it too seriously, like you always do." Ian had always worn his heart on his sleeve. No one was surprised when he decided to go to medical school and even less surprised when he announced that he wanted to practice psychiatry.

Samantha broke his reverie into their past by rolling over in bed to face him. "We're going to do this, Ian. I promise. Violet is so happy there. I'm not going to let them ruin her life over a little money."

"I know. I was just remembering how much I admire you." Ian gazed at her for a moment. A sliver of moonlight lit her cheekbone. "You're the best wife—the best mother. We're all lucky to have you."

"The best mother? Ha! I may have gotten them all grown, but I can't manage them. Lukas is doing well, at least." Their oldest son was finishing his Ph.D. in archeology at the University of Southern California. Mitchell was finally getting his life together and was enrolled at a smaller liberal arts school to get a degree in art education.

"You're wonderful," Ian said, smoothing Samantha's chin-length hair behind her ear. He fell asleep with his hand still on her neck.

The next morning, Samantha gathered the file of paperwork she'd collected from PWHO while she was there with Violet over the weekend. She'd collected letters from Yvonne, the director of PWHO; Lauren, the clinical coordinator; Kelly, Violet's house manager; Dr. Hendrix, the psychiatrist who worked with the Prader-Willi clients; and from other relevant staff. She took a deep breath and started digging through various websites to find an intake worker with the state who could help her push Violet's application through.

•••

At his office, Ian's first phone call was to Mrs. Posey, to tell her they'd received the letter and to ask if she had any recommendations for people who could help them navigate the state system. She was able to make several recommendations.

Ian spent the next week making exhausting phone calls, one after the other, to numerous potential resources, some of whom were more helpful than others. He finally got the name and number of an attorney, Don Harris, who he was told had worked with many families that had children with disabilities.

Monday of the next week, Ian made his first phone call with a stomach full of butterflies. Don Harris answered on the first ring.

"Hi, Don. This is Ian Durkin. My daughter, Violet, is currently in placement at Prader-Willi Homes of Oconomowoc," Ian started. And then he proceeded to tell him the whole story.

"Is she turning twenty-one?" Don asked. His tone was compassionate—obviously he had to be as a special needs attorney—but not without an edge that indicated he could dominate a courtroom.

"She will be, in one year," Ian replied. "How did you know?"

"It's my job. How may I be of service to you?"

"The school district funding is ending in a year. We need assistance with getting the state to see things from our perspective. We are hoping she can stay at PWHO," Ian said.

"This happens all the time. The school board has borne the funding burden because Violet is under twenty-one and has the right to a free and appropriate education. When she reaches twenty-one, she is no longer eligible for special education services, so protections under special education law no longer apply. Although she still needs funding and help, it is now the responsibility of the adult system to determine eligibility and fund services and placement. There is another law, the Americans with Disabilities Act, that provides some protection for people with disabilities, but it isn't very specific. It covers wishes more than needs for a fulfilled and successful life," Don replied. "But there are defined agencies at the state level charged with the responsibility of providing services and funding for people with disabilities. There are different agencies that deal with different types of disabilities. The first step is to identify the appropriate agency and work through getting her eligible for services. Then comes securing the funding."

"So what does that mean?" Ian asked, dread creeping into his voice.

"Well, it depends. Do you have a state social worker?" Don asked.

"Not yet," Ian replied. "My wife's been working on that for a week and is working on that again today."

"Don't worry about it. When I file all the paperwork, the state will assign you one. Now, what I need you to do is collect letters from every expert who has ever worked with Violet. We need new letters from each of the professionals, even those who haven't worked with her for years. In addition, we need letters from each of the experts at PWHO. That evidence is how we make the state see things our way."

"I have those letters. I can definitely work on getting new letters from her old therapists and teachers from high school," Ian said. "But what good will new letters do when they haven't had any interaction with Violet at all since she's been at PWHO?"

"It will contrast the difference in her with and without the level of care at PWHO. What's probably going to happen is that the state is going to insist that Violet move back home with some kind of community-based care. Their goal is to provide services that are the least restrictive. Home is the least restrictive option. They will offer you what's called 'in-home community-based services,' meaning they'll send someone into your home to provide therapy for Vi, behavior management systems for you, and other things. If that doesn't work, they'll agree to provide respite care at home, which would involve someone from an approved respite provider agency coming to give you and Sam a break twice a week or so. The next step would be to find a residential facility in state. There are a couple of homes they'll recommend. You need to visit those homes and decide if they would be a good fit for Violet. Chances are, they're not equipped to serve someone with Prader-Willi, and when you bring them copies of letters detailing Violet's necessary level of care, most of them will say that they can't treat her. The last option that the state will want you to take is keeping her in out-of-state residential care. That's PWHO, where Violet is now. We need to convince the state that she is thriving there like she won't anywhere else." Don was an old pro.

"Well, that's the truth," Ian added.

"Yes, well, you have quite a job ahead of you. I'll file all the necessary paperwork with the state, but it's going to be up to you to collect it, and you and your wife will have to draft letters from your perspective, too. We want as much tangible evidence as possible convincing the state that Violet needs to stay at PWHO," Don said.

"I can do that. Anything for Violet to maintain her happy life. She really loves it there, you know," Ian said quietly. He could feel tears pricking the backs of his eyes.

"I know," Don said. "Look, there are no promises, except the one that I'll deliver now: we're going to do everything that we can to keep Violet there." Don's normally professional tone wavered for just a moment, and the fact that he'd devoted his entire career to helping families with special needs hit Ian hard.

"Thank you, Don. Can we discuss your retainer?" Ian asked, ever the pragmatist.

"Ah, that part. Is it okay if I have my assistant send you an email with that?" Don had a bit of a chuckle in his voice.

"Sure. Not like it matters, really. We need all the help that we can get. I'll also get the letters that I already have faxed to you this morning," Ian said, making note of the deliverables he promised him.

"Sounds good. Thanks."

"Thank you." Ian hung up the phone, for a moment overwhelmed by the work that was facing him. He quickly shook it off, took a deep breath, and called Samantha. She was working at home today, and he wanted her to get those letters faxed to Don Harris's office as soon as she could.

. . .

Samantha poured herself a second cup of coffee. It had been two weeks since they received the letter from the school district, and the letters Marilyn promised had finally arrived. She gathered the papers and went to Ian's office to fax over the lot, ten pages, to Don's office. As she was starting to fax them, she read over Marilyn's letter.

To the State Department of Human Services:

As the admissions director at PWHO, I've been working with Violet Durkin for two and a half years. Violet has Prader-Willi Syndrome. She cannot control her eating, and her weight was escalating out of control—two hundred and thirty-three pounds on her five-foot frame—when I met her. At that time, she bordered on paranoia and was agitated and extremely volatile. She was prone to aggression and acted out frequently.

Through our intensive program that includes healthy balanced meals locked in a kitchen until meal or snack time, a vigorous and consistent activity program, as well as socialization and individual and group therapy, Violet has shown great improvements in her behavior. These improvements will only continue to work if she remains in a stabilized environment that offers specialized treatment for her specific syndrome.

My ongoing concern for Violet is that she cannot control her eating. This is a direct effect of Prader-Willi Syndrome and a primary symptom. This could lead to cardiopulmonary crises, compromised diabetes control, and other metabolic dysregulation issues, all of which could become life threatening if she doesn't reside in a structured environment with external controls on her caloric intake. Most agencies not familiar with treating Prader-Willi Syndrome are unable to manage this potentially life-threatening condition successfully.

I'd be happy to set up a time to talk with you at more length about Violet's syndrome and who she is as a person. Please feel free to contact me.

Respectfully,
Marilyn Jackson

Samantha's eyes welled with tears reading through Marilyn's letter. Although it was pretty general and she discussed the characteristics typical of all people with Prader-Willi Syndrome, the fact that she cared enough to sit down and write it at all touched Samantha in a way she hadn't expected. She knew she could be tough—she had to be, in her career—but she had a real soft spot for anyone who loved her children. The people at PWHO fit that bill.

After contacting Dr. Kraemer, Violet's former psychiatrist, Violet's special education advocate from the school district, her pediatrician at Pine View, and Mrs. Posey, Samantha had to settle her mind that she'd done everything she could that day. She went into her bathroom and ran a hot shower, trying to wash away the fear that everything might not be okay for Violet forever.

Two weeks passed, and Samantha and Ian hadn't heard anything from anyone, except Don. He called every three days or so to let the Durkins know that he'd received another letter or had filed a petition with the state. He'd told Samantha and Ian to let him speak with the social worker, that their job was to collect information and let him deal with it. God, the paperwork—Ian hadn't written so much or signed his name so often since he was in residency, and Samantha was growing weary of calling to remind and nudge elementary school teachers, doctors' offices, and therapists that Violet hadn't worked with in fifteen years to please submit a letter. She was more than happy to let Don do his job, but her lack of control over the process was making her crazy. She'd distracted herself with work, but her anxiety constantly made her worry about the involved process that was happening in the backstage area of her life. When her cell phone rang on a Thursday afternoon, showing an unfamiliar number, she didn't know what to expect.

"Mrs. Durkin? This is Nicholas Livingston from the state."

"Hi, Nicholas." Samantha's voice conveyed the unease the phone call brought her. *This must be the social worker assigned by the state.*

"I've been working with your attorney, Don Harris, on Violet's case for the past two weeks, and I'm calling you with an update. I hope that you don't mind, but I'm *your* social worker, your advocate. You and I are on the same side." His voice was young and smooth, a baritone that would have been more suited on an old R&B album than a young man calling about state funding.

"Sure, Mr. Livingston. What's going on?" Samantha asked, put more at ease by the young man's reassurances.

"Nick, please. I understand that you'd like to keep Violet in her current placement, and between you and I, I don't blame you. She seems to be having a lot of success there. However, it is my duty to report three homes that can work with her syndrome in the state. The state understands that respite care at home just won't work for her." Samantha could hear the smile in his voice.

Samantha gave a silent sigh of relief. She wasn't sure if it was the work of Nick or Don, but she was grateful for the team she had. This wasn't the answer that she'd expected from the state, and starting three steps ahead of where she'd anticipated was a blessing.

"Thank you, Nick," Samantha said.

"So, I'll email you the information on the homes—there are three of them, and I'd like for you and your husband to check them out as soon as you can. Of course, we don't want to send your daughter anywhere that doesn't have your blessing." Nick said, comfortingly.

How things have changed, thought Samantha, bitterly recalling the home that the state had placed Violet in when she was eighteen. Although Nick's voice was kind, Samantha could tell that he was hoping that she'd agree to an in-state program instead of PWHO. She'd worked in business long enough to know this negotiating tactic—if they made an offer of care, it would be harder for the family to refuse and continue fighting for the program that their daughter deserved.

"Please, send them over. I'm sure my husband and I can find time to visit them next week," Samantha said positively.

"I'm glad to hear that. Expect that info in your inbox shortly. It was great to talk to you. I hope that we can do it again." Nick's voice was professional but kind. Samantha got a feeling that he was passionate about his work, and that comforted her.

After her last meeting of the day, Samantha got straight into her car and drove home. Ian had the afternoon off, and she wanted to catch him up on what she and Nick had discussed. She also needed to get her hands on his calendar to make the time for viewing the homes next week.

"Hey, baby," Ian said, when his wife came in through the garage door. He was sitting at the dining table with his laptop.

"Hey, yourself. How was your day?" She leaned down to give him a kiss.

"It was actually pretty good. I have some notes to get to Karin to transcribe, but otherwise I've been pretty open all afternoon. How was your day?" he asked.

"Well, Nicholas Livingston, our state social worker, called me today," Samantha started. She could see Ian's brow furrow. "It wasn't bad news. It was actually better than expected. He wants us to start checking out homes here—"

"So they want to move Violet out of PWHO. Of course!" Ian was furious.

"No, baby. Remember, Don talked us through this. This is a step that we all have to take in order to ensure her funding. It is required that the state investigate all in-state options before they can allow an out-of-state place-ment. Since Prader-Willi is so specific, if we can rule these out, the only logical step to take is to keep her at PWHO."

Ian half-smiled. "Oh, yeah. I see."

"So, Nick emailed me three possible placements. What day next week can you take off to check these out with me?" Samantha handed Ian the copy of the email she'd printed just before she left the office.

"You want to see them all in a day?" Ian looked at the list skeptically. "Sam, these are all over the state."

"Well, let's take two days. I want to get this settled as quickly as possible. We can't afford to run out of time and have to pay for Violet's care ourselves, in addition to Don's fees . . ."

Ian pulled turned to his laptop. "It looks like Tuesday and Wednesday can be rearranged to accommodate two free days. What about you?"

"Whatever. I'll do what I have to do to my schedule. Let's just get on the road, partner." Samantha smiled at Ian. They were going to do this, and they were going to do it together.

. . .

From the moment the Durkins drove up to the first home, Samantha knew that it wasn't going to work for Violet. While they were told the home was "just minutes from Capitol City," they'd driven a full hour outside of the city. The area was rural, and it had been at least twenty minutes since Samantha had even seen a gas station. This was the polar opposite of Oconomowoc, where the community was open to the residents of PWHO. That allowed Violet and the other residents to have jobs in the community, giving them a sense of importance and belonging to a network bigger than their own residential organization. Without that, Samantha was sure Violet would feel lonely and discarded. Worse, when they approached the white brick building, Samantha was sure that she'd seen it on one of the ghost shows that Mitchell used to watch in high school. It looked like an old, haunted house, complete with the ornate iron gates that Disney World had on the Haunted Mansion ride. Ian pulled their car around to the front parking lot and shot Samantha a skeptical look before unbuckling his seatbelt.

"Do we have to go inside? It's eerie," Ian said, only half joking.

"Might as well get this out of the way," Samantha said. "Let's hope it's a quick visit."

At the front desk, they were greeted by a woman with big red hair, which she fluffed with fingers adorned with long acrylic fingernails.

"We're Dr. and Mrs. Durkin. We have an admissions meeting with Pauline regarding our daughter, Violet," Ian said.

"Oh, yes! So sorry, I had you down for nine-thirty. Give me just a minute. We're all running a little behind today, anyway." The woman—Pauline, evidently—gave an embarrassed smile. Samantha was certain that they'd agreed on nine. She even had the email confirming the time that Pauline had sent her. Besides, what did "behind" mean? Violet's scheduling needs were so specific that if "running a little behind" was typical, her daughter wouldn't thrive here.

"Come with me," Pauline said, after disappearing into an office and leaving Samantha and Ian standing by the front door. They looked around the lobby, which smelled clean, though the tile betrayed years of hard use that no amount of mopping or waxing would fix.

"This is the kitchen," Pauline said, gesturing toward double swinging doors as they passed. "We—"

"Wait a second." Ian stopped her. "This is the entrance to the kitchen? These doors? Everyone can get inside?"

"Well, yes," Pauline said, smiling uncertainly. "We like to think that we're a family here. No room is off-limits to our residents."

"This is already not going to work," Ian said. "Our daughter has Prader-Willi Syndrome. Are you familiar with that?"

"Oh, sure. Like Down's syndrome?" Pauline asked.

"No. The only thing the two have in common is that they are both genetic disorders. The primary characteristic of Prader-Willi is an inability to ever feel satiated. Therefore, our daughter is in a constant search for food. Violet needs to be somewhere where the food is locked up and out of her reach. Otherwise, she could quite literally eat herself to death."

Pauline raised one of her penciled eyebrows. "Dr. Durkin, respectfully, we can't run a house where our residents don't have access to food. That's a violation of our licensing. We have successfully treated residents with bi-polar, autism, and Down's syndrome, and we've never had an issue. I can assure you that—"

"We understand," Samantha said, cutting off Pauline and taking over for Ian, who was indignant. "So, this place, while I'm sure it provides a high quality of life for its residents, isn't going to work for Violet's specific needs. Could you write a letter for us to the state stating that?"

"Well . . . I . . ." Pauline stuttered, taken aback by the request.

"It's not just that she can't have access to the kitchen; it's that she is an avid food seeker," Samantha explained. "She will use anything available to her to get to the food, even with it locked up. Manipulation, violence, tantrums . . ." Samantha trailed off, hoping that by naming some of Violet's worst tendencies she'd scare Pauline into writing the letter stating that her facility couldn't provide services to Violet.

"Oh, we're used to all those things here. We're specially equipped to deal with patients who aren't . . . flexible," Pauline said. Her pause before choosing the word *flexible* made Ian sick to his stomach. This woman had no idea how to handle a resident with Prader-Willi, and after the bad experience that they'd had with the first home into which Violet was placed, he wasn't fooling around with this anymore.

"Violet has very specific medical needs as well. The tricky thing about her is that she has an IQ of sixty-nine—so she's aware of everything, and she often gets frustrated and confused if she's taken off a schedule or if she's not treated with the specific interventions that she needs. Violet has OCD, and her anxiety can get so high that she picks her skin and pulls out her own hair. She also has bouts of explosive diarrhea and occasional bowel obstructions, and these things require hospitalization, not a normal wait-and-see approach." Ian saw the look of horror come over Pauline's face and knew that he and Samantha had thoroughly convinced her that her facility wasn't right for Violet.

"Okay, I hate to say this, but I don't think that we would be the best fit for Violet . . ." Pauline trailed off.

"Great! We'll just go sit in the lobby while you draft that letter. Thank you so much for your time, Pauline. We won't bother you anymore once we get that letter from you." Samantha put on her dazzling PR smile and started to lead the group back towards the front office.

Half an hour later, Ian and Samantha were back in their car and ready to move on to the next home.

"We have time for an early lunch before heading to the next one." Samantha smiled at Ian. Everything felt more complete after getting one third of the remaining material.

Three hours passed before Ian pulled up to the second residential facility. As he was driving up the road, he got chills down his spine. He knew this place. He looked at the name and address again on his GPS. The name may have changed, but when he saw the building, he wanted to turn the car around right there.

"This is where Violet was first," he said to Samantha, in little more than a whisper.

"My God. You're right." Samantha sat dead in her seat. "Well, we're certainly not sending her back here. We've already had disastrous results. I was thinking that it was a new facility—not just the same place with a new name." She unbuckled her seatbelt. "At least this will be easy. They've already failed. I'm going to pop in and get a letter."

"You sure?" Ian's voice was strained.

"Yep. I got this. Let me go in. I won't get emotional.

I promise." Samantha leaned over and gave her husband a quick peck on the lips before getting out of the car.

He watched his wife walk in and felt his body tingling as he recalled Violet's previous stay there . . . her alarmingly quick weight gain and the misery in her normally bright eyes. He just couldn't imagine putting her through that again. He hated himself for allowing it to happen the first time. His eyes welled with tears as he thought back to those sleepless nights when all he could think about was how he'd been entrusted with this angel, and he couldn't make it right. He could provide the best schools and birthday parties, pony rides and video games—but not a safe place to live as an adult. The thought broke his heart. He was so happy that Violet had found such success, and he gave thanks each night for the loving people who were taking care of his little girl. He couldn't imagine having Violet stay in a place like this again, even temporarily.

Just then, the passenger's door opened and Samantha was grinning from ear to ear. "Got it!" she said, waving a sheet of paper.

"What?" Ian's eyes widened.

"I explained to them who I was and why I was there. They couldn't get me a letter and get me out of there fast enough." Samantha smiled. "They knew they couldn't handle her again, and thank God, they didn't want to try."

Ian was almost trembling with relief. He didn't even want this to be on the table as an option. Didn't the state keep a record of the last time Violet was there? At least Samantha was doing what she could to keep moving through the process. She was better with these situations than he was.

The next morning, Samantha and Ian woke up in their hotel room, which overlooked a big river. They were in a small town close to the state border, their final stop on the tour of residential facilities that the state had outlined for them to check out in their appeal to keep Violet's funding for services at PWHO.

They drove around the area, and it was nice enough. Just another small town in the river valley. Violet would be about the same distance from home here as she was in Wisconsin, and who knew? While the Durkins wanted to keep Violet where she was comfortable, at least there was some hope that if she had to leave, she could possibly be somewhere comparable.

Ian guided his car down the winding path that led to the facility. A beautiful white picket fence surrounded the property as far as they could see. The branches of tall trees moved slightly in the wind, and the sun poked over the riverbank in greeting, casting a surreal yellow light off the white house with immaculate siding. The front yard was covered in raised gardens, and Samantha could see handwritten signs indicating where the broccoli, green beans, and tomatoes were planted. *This is cute,* she thought, although the idea of Violet handling food worried her a little.

Ian followed Samantha onto the expansive front porch and through the glass doors that opened into a lobby. The house smelled like his grandmother's—a musky perfume mixed with Pine cleaner. The unique combination triggered a part of his brain, reminding him of his youth out at her house.

"You must be the Durkins!" A round, older lady waddled around from the other side of the main desk.

"We are," Samantha smiled, extending her hand. "I'm Samantha, and this is my husband, Ian."

"It's so nice to meet you! My name is Janette, and I'm the admissions director. We're a small operation here, because today I'm also in charge of the front desk." The lady giggled, and it was then that Samantha realized the resemblance she bore to the blue fairy in Sleeping Beauty. She was round and grey and adorable. All she needed was a blue cape with a hood.

"Well, we're just pleased to have you here!" Janette's accent betrayed that she wasn't from the Midwest.

"Where are you from?" Samantha asked.

"Oh, my voice does it every time," Janette laughed. "I was born and raised in Louisiana."

Samantha and Ian felt warmth from her, and as she led them around her facilities, they took turns explaining the modifications that Violet would need due to her syndrome. Janette patiently listened and gave her thoughts on how she could arrange those things. After the tour, the three of them sat at a round table off the lobby.

"I guess the only thing that bothers me is that Violet has a job where she lives now. She loves the idea of working and being independent. How could that translate here?" Samantha asked.

"Well, our residents work, too!" Janette exclaimed. "By golly, we're a community, and we all have to contribute."

"Right now she's doing quality control for a company in Oconomowoc. What would she be doing here?" Ian chimed in.

"I'm glad you asked! We have a contract with the hospital. Our higher functioning residents are able to serve food in the cafeteria and bring meals to patients' rooms.

It's a really wonderful arrangement."

Samantha sighed. It was as if she hadn't just spent the past hour and a half explaining Prader-Willi Syndrome to Janette.

"Violet can't have unrestricted access to food, Janette."

"Well, it wouldn't be unrestricted. People would be watching her."

"I don't think you understand." Samantha could feel her tethers rising. "Violet can't have *any* contact with food that she isn't supposed to eat. When food is around, she goes into a primal drive state. She can't control herself, regardless of who's watching. It's like asking a recovering alcoholic to tend bar. Not a good situation to put our daughter in."

Janette looked at Samantha as if she was speaking Chinese. "Huh. Well, I'm sure we could just work something out when she got here."

"No. That won't work. Janette, you seem wonderful. We're impressed with your setup here, but Violet's syndrome is so unique and rare that I don't think you're equipped to handle her—at no fault of your own." Samantha smiled sympathetically.

Janette looked uncomfortable. "I think you're right. I hate that. I really do. I want to help everyone who needs it."

"We have Violet in a perfect program right now. It's in Wisconsin, and the state prefers that she move back to an in-state facility. The biggest help that you could give us is a letter stating that you can't appropriately manage Violet here. Our attorney and advocate for the state will use that letter to try and ensure that Violet can stay where she is indefinitely." Samantha thought that honesty was the best policy. She smiled at Janette, having just poured her heart out before the woman.

Janette returned that smile. "Let's go into my office, and I'll write the letter."

"Perfect." Samantha smiled that perfect PR smile while Ian sat in amazement. Samantha always knew exactly how to get people to do what she wanted, and in this case, he couldn't be happier that she was using her power for their daughter.

"Let me make a quick phone call before you come in here." Janette smiled at the Durkins and led them to the lobby while she stepped into her office and shut the door.

"I can't believe this was so easy!" Ian looked at Samantha. "Leave it to you!" He grinned and put his hand on her knee. They were so close to getting this tucked away with Don and Nick to do their work.

A few minutes later, Janette emerged from her office. Her happy demeanor had changed. "I'm so sorry," she said, avoiding eye contact with Samantha. "I won't be able to write that letter for you."

"What? Why not?" Samantha rose to her feet.

"Well, I just talked to my manager, and he says that we'll be able to make all of the necessary adjustments to fit Violet's needs. He's actually planning on expanding this program to include Prader-Willi Syndrome clients. He's even working out a training program with Oconomowoc." Janette smiled.

Samantha was skeptical and beginning to get angry. "My daughter was a guinea pig once, and it's not going to happen again. We are not sure you can effectively manage her syndrome, and you've pretty much agreed with that. We're not confident that the 'necessary adjustments' will work. We don't trust that they will!"

"Mrs. Durkin, if you would just calm down a moment, you will see that—"

"I will not calm down. My daughter will not live here!" Samantha was livid. She turned to Ian, who was still sitting. "Let's go."

She marched out of the office, determined to fight this pseudo-placement with everything she had.

As soon as she got home, Samantha wrote letters to Don and Nick, detailing her experience at the third home and why it wasn't suitable for Violet. She mentioned the food availability, the lack of a scheduled routine, and the lack of daily activity—all of which were important for Violet's physical and emotional health. She emailed the letters and crossed her fingers that her word would be enough to convince the state that Violet didn't need to be moved from PWHO. She then poured herself a rather full glass of wine and read a celebrity magazine until she fell asleep, still clothed, across the bed. She just couldn't find it in herself to do anything else.

CHAPTER 16

The next morning, Samantha awoke feeling more than a little hungover. She looked at her nightstand, where the glass of wine she'd poured the night before was still mostly intact. She was rubbing her temples when it hit her: clearly, she was experiencing an emotional hangover. The thought made her scoff a little as she rolled out of her bed and ran a hot shower.

Beneath the soothing water, Samantha felt near tears again when she remembered the day before. Now what? When Janette's manager refused to allow her to write the letter, Samantha's dreams for her daughter were dashed. The Department of Human Services wanted to keep her in the state, and it would be her word against the facility's that it just wasn't *right* for her daughter. Violet would have to live in a home that was unable to meet her needs, potentially putting her at life-threatening risk, just so she could satisfy the state. Samantha shuddered to imagine Violet being asked to serve food. That was the same as putting a loaded gun in her hand; it was only a matter of time before a slip of movement pulled the trigger.

After her shower, Samantha pulled a soft tennis dress over her head and sent an email to her assistant, telling her that she'd be out another day. Samantha hadn't called in so often since Violet lived at home. Everything was colliding around her—there was a shift in the tectonic plates that threatened to smash Samantha between mountains that she just couldn't climb. After a moment of consideration, she pulled the comforter down from the made bed and crawled back underneath. She was reveling in the warmth when her cell phone rang.

"Samantha Durkin," she answered flatly.

"It's Don Harris. I got your email. So did Nicholas."

"And?" She was just too tired to give any sort of polite response.

"Good news: Violet has been awarded funding as an adult. Bad news: it's at the respite home that you've detailed as bad for her."

"What the hell, Don?" Samantha was exhausted, so her words were stronger than her inflection.

"I know. This isn't going to work for anyone," Don said.

"So what do we do now? I'm not sending Violet there next year. She can't come home." Samantha's voice grew frantic.

"Now is the time to take drastic measures." Don's voice was steady. "There are still no promises, but here's what I propose: Take the letter that you wrote to Nicholas and me last night and forward it to Marjorie, to Nick's boss, and to your state representative and your congressman. While we're waiting for responses from them, I'm going to file a suit to appeal against the state. We've proven that Violet was eligible for services from the school district for a long time and that she deserves the funding. We've also proven that there is nowhere in the state that can treat her effectively, regardless of what this home is saying they *might* be able to do for her with substantial changes to their program. The ruling of the Department of Human Services is not in Violet's best interests, and I think we have a case."

"Suing the state? That's your recommendation?" Samantha was dumbstruck by his suggestion; however, if he thought they had a snowball's chance in hell of winning it, she was in. "Okay. I'm game. Let me get the ball rolling on my side. You do the same on yours."

After hanging up, she collected her laptop from the bedside table and moved into the kitchen to review what she'd sent Don and Nick the night before. She edited the material for the updates she'd just received from Don and then reread it, the gravity of the situation pulling her down to the lowest she'd been since before Violet had gone to live at PWHO.

To Whom it May Concern:

My daughter, Violet Durkin, has been a resident at Prader-Willi Homes of Oconomowoc for two years now. Not just any group home would do for her since her syndrome is so rare that specialized services are critical to her well-being. At the request of the Department of Human Services, I've checked every recommended residential facility in the state and come up empty-handed for a solution.

PWHO was, and continues to be, our salvation. They had an opening for an immediate placement when Violet was eighteen. We were not only able to continue her education with vocational training, but her needs were taken care of by the specialized services specific to Prader-Willi that are provided on campus.

Upon Violet's twenty-first birthday, the school district will no longer provide the necessary funding for Violet's placement at PWHO. We have applied for adult placement through DHS in order to continue her funding and were told that we had to move our child from her home to an in-state facility. Not only were the limited facilities in this state inappropriate, but the state is also clearly unfamiliar with Prader-Willi Syndrome. However, by word of my attorney, Don Harris, Violet was proven eligible for funding, but the state refuses to budge on the issue of providing her care where she is currently.

As a mother, I want my child to live the best, most full life that she can. I'm sure if you're a parent, you can relate. Please, consider my appeal of this decision before my family is forced to take further legal action in protection of our child.

Respectfully,
Samantha Durkin

Satisfied with the letter, she took a deep breath before sending three copies to the printer.

The next three months were sheer torture. Don filed the appeal, and Samantha worked to get all of the valid information to him; but to her great surprise, she found that filing the paperwork justifying the appeal was the worst part. She had to collect additional letters from Violet's staff at PWHO, as well as her old psychologist, psychiatrist, speech therapist, occupational therapist, and former high school teachers. They had to produce documentation rebutting the claims made by the in-state facility that they would take care of Violet's very particular needs. Don had to walk her and Ian through the procedures of the Department of Human Services so that they could look for criteria, eligibility definitions, administrative codes, and department policies and procedures that were applicable to Violet's case. Samantha had to build a case for appropriate treatment to fulfill Violet's very specific, unique needs; for the imaginative solutions to Violet's problems, such as the very short haircut; and the substantial weight loss that Violet had experienced during her stay at Prader-Willi Homes of Oconomowoc. Ian researched the toll on Violet's health that would have been taken over the past two years if she'd remained at two hundred and thirty-three pounds. He found evidence that she would probably suffer with gout, hypertension, and cardiopulmonary distress, and shared the fact that she'd begun to menstruate, indicating an improvement in her previously nonexistent reproductive health.

Each time either Samantha or Ian's phones rang or their emails dinged, their stomachs lurched to the back of their throats—the potential impending bad news shook Samantha to her core. Did she need to come up with something else? Had they just flat-out decided that Violet had to be moved in state?

The Durkins had filed all their necessary paperwork, and Don advised them to sit and wait until they could get a court date. One afternoon, Samantha just couldn't take the waiting game anymore and came home from work a little early. She was exhausted and looking forward to a nap, but she found that Ian was waiting for her.

"Surprise!" he said when she walked through the door.

"Surprise, what?" Samantha asked warily.

"Surprise! We're going out tonight! You don't have to

look fancy. Just bring yourself."

Samantha looked at Ian, who had changed out of his typical work attire of a button-down shirt, pressed khakis, and brown loafers into cargo shorts, a polo shirt, and sandals. Samantha went into her room to change into a sundress and sandals. She clipped the front of her short hair up in a barrette and grabbed her purse.

"I'm ready." She smiled as she looked into her husband's eyes. Just because the last few months had been torturous didn't mean they shouldn't do something fun, something for them.

Ian grabbed an insulated bag and his wife's hand before leading her a few blocks to a local park where the kids used to play when they were young. Away from the playground was a nice, open meadow—an oasis from the city life that bustled around them. He pulled a blanket from the bag and encouraged Samantha to have a seat while he poured two glasses of champagne.

"How sweet," Samantha said when Ian was beside her.

"To us, forever," Ian responded, clinking his plastic cup to hers.

"Oh, God," Samantha said out loud.

"What?" Ian's asked, concerned.

"Today is our anniversary. I can't believe I—I'm so sorry, Ian." Samantha lowered her eyes. She'd been married for twenty-nine years, and in the midst of all the drama with Violet's funding situation, she'd completely forgotten.

"It's okay, Sam. Really. I didn't remember until you sent me the text that you were taking off early. I wasn't sure if it was a test, so I threw together this picnic as quickly as I could." Ian's ears were turning red. "So it wasn't a test?"

Samantha laughed. "Not at all, but I'm glad it worked out. God, we were just babies then." She laid her head in her husband's lap and looked up into his dark eyes, his hair that was quickly becoming more salt than pepper. What was it about men—getting more handsome as their faces matured with age?

Ian brushed Samantha's ever-lighter hair from her face and returned her gaze. "We thought we knew everything then, huh? I was twenty-eight, and you were . . ."

"I was twenty-six, barely. You were in your residency, and I moved here to take the city by storm after finishing up at business school." Samantha smiled nostalgically, remembering that ambitious young woman who could do anything.

"*Harvard* Business School, you were quick to tell anyone who asked. Or didn't," Ian said through a clenched jaw, mocking the blue-bloodedness of her Ivy League experience. She jokingly swatted at him.

"This is so nice," she said softly. "Us . . . spending time together like this. I've always loved you, but it's been easy to forget just how much I *like* you with everything else going on."

"I know. So much for the golden years," Ian said, half-jokingly.

Samantha laughed. "I don't know about you, sir, but I am quite happy being the young and vivacious one in this relationship."

Ian started to protest, but he was interrupted by the ringing of Samantha's cell phone. She couldn't decide whether to throw it across the park or answer it. When she saw Don Harris's number flash across her screen, she answered.

"Samantha Durkin." She put one finger up to Ian, indicating that it was an important call. Ian looked glum anyway; it was a rejection that he took personally.

"Yes, hi, Don." She emphasized the attorney's name so Ian knew exactly why she had to take the call. Ian perked up a little, listening carefully to Samantha's side of the conversation.

"Really? Do we need to do anything? What's going to happen now?" Samantha was nodding her head vigorously, making Ian even more anxious about the conversation. "Well, great. Thanks so much, Don. Keep us informed over the next week. Bye now."

She ended the call on her cell phone and looked at Ian before she burst squarely into tears.

Ian felt a chill, despite the warm afternoon. He knew that Violet would have to move to the new facility. Why did Don have to call with bad news when they'd just . . .

Samantha broke Ian's swirl of negativity when she spoke through her tears. "I'm just so relieved. The lawsuit worked. Finally. Don just got a call from the attorney from the Department of Human Services. They're willing to settle outside of court. Don will be in negotiations with them by the end of the week!"

"So what does this mean?" Ian exclaimed.

"It means that they are willing to pay for Violet to stay in Wisconsin when her school funding stops at her twenty-first birthday. They don't want to be tied up in court over this for possibly years. That means we won't have to figure out how to pay for what's best for Violet." The last few words that Samantha spoke rang in her ears: *what's best for Violet*. She had been so overwhelmed with this process that she'd temporarily lost touch with what she was fighting for: her daughter, the little girl who'd started life as a fragile flower but since blossomed into a complex, resilient, loving woman. Samantha was overcome with gratitude.

CHAPTER 17

Beep, beep, beep. Violet opened her eyes, but could barely make out the numbers on her digital clock without her glasses. She knew that they read five-thirty, since that was always the time that she awoke, but instead of hitting the snooze button and rolling over, like normal, she sat straight up. Today wasn't just a normal day; it was her birthday.

"It's my birthday. I'm twenty-one," Violet called out to her roommate, Stephanie.

A muffled giggle came from the three pillows that Stephanie insisted on sleeping with each night. Her roommate rustled a little under her comforter, but Violet knew that she wasn't going to get out of bed until the snooze alarm rang at five thirty-nine. Violet rolled from bed and collected her things for her shower. There was always a set schedule for the showers, with each resident getting one in either the morning or the evening. Violet always showered in the morning, but since today was her birthday, she'd requested the first shower, which meant that she needed to get to the bathroom early.

She quietly padded down the hallway in her socks, trying not to wake anyone who wasn't already up. She turned the knob on the door, only to find it locked.

"Who's in there?" she demanded. "I get the first shower today! Suzanne told everyone at dinner! It's my birthday, and it's on the schedule!"

"I was up first." Gwen's voice came from the other side of the locked bathroom door. "I got here first. It's only fair."

Violet's face heated up at the injustice. She hit the door with all her might. "I get the first shower today! It was on the schedule! You're always taking things away from other people, Gwen! You're such a bitch!"

"What's going on, Violet?" Wendy, the morning staff member, came up behind Violet and put her hands on her shoulders.

"Today is my birthday, and I was scheduled to have the first shower!" Violet shrieked. "Gwen went into the bathroom early, and she's hogging all the hot water. She got the first shower, and it just isn't fair! She didn't follow the schedule. She *knew* I was supposed to get here first!"

"No, Violet, it wasn't fair. I'll have a talk with Gwen about following the schedule, but for now, you need to collect yourself a little. It's your birthday, and you don't want to start the day off sad, do you?" Wendy tilted her head at Violet.

Violet started to sob. "I don't, but now it's too late. My whole day is already ruined. I'll only get the second shower. This is the *worst* birthday, ever!"

Violet pulled away from Wendy and ran back into her room, slamming the door. She pulled the covers over her head and tried to collect enough hair to pull. Since she'd kept the pixie cut for the past few years, she couldn't grasp enough of it to yank, and that further frustrated her. She heard the door close, indicating that Stephanie had left her alone, and she felt like no one loved her. It was her birthday—and no one cared that she was upset. She howled, curling up in her bed. Suddenly the world was so dark, and Violet couldn't do anything about it. She heard someone come in and put a chair by the side of her bed, and peeked out of her covers to see Kelly sitting there.

"Violet, what's wrong?" Kelly asked.

"Gwen took the first shower when I was supposed to have it. It's my birthday, and it's just not fair," Violet said from under the covers.

"It's not fair, but what's something that we talk about a lot?" Kelly asked calmly.

"Life's not fair?" Violet said.

"No. I've never said that to you," Kelly said. "When things aren't fair, we use our words to talk to our friends about why we feel that things are unfair. We all care about each other, and no one wants to hurt anyone else. Gwen owes you an apology, but you also owe her and Wendy one for the way that you talked to them."

Violet looked out. "But it wasn't fair," she insisted in a smaller voice.

"It wasn't, but you didn't make it any better with your actions," Kelly said.

Violet sighed huffily. She knew that Kelly was right.

"Now, you've run out of time for a lot of things and you will have to hurry to make breakfast," Kelly said. "Would you like to apologize first and ask Wendy to hold the bathroom for you so that you can get in and out?"

Violet nodded, gathered her things, and walked down the hallway. Wendy was still standing outside the bathroom door.

"I'm sorry, Wendy," Violet said, looking down. "Sometimes I just get so mad, but I'm embarrassed that I talked to you like that."

"I know, Violet. I accept your apology. I saved the bathroom for you."

"Thank you, Wendy." Violet smiled as she walked into the bathroom, closing the door behind herself.

After her shower, Violet was excited to use the birthday present that her parents had sent the weekend before. Since they were coming up the following weekend to watch her play basketball instead of this weekend for her birthday, they'd mailed her a package and let her open it early—but Violet had been patient and hadn't used a thing. Now she slathered the vanilla cupcake lotion all over her skin, dressed in her new top, and stood in the mirror to apply the finishing touch: pink lip gloss. The lip gloss tasted like watermelon and left a perfect shine. Violet was finally ready for her twenty-first birthday to begin.

Violet was the last to arrive at the table for breakfast, but she was still on time. She sat by Gwen and gave her a hug. "I'm sorry," she whispered into Gwen's ear.

"Me, too," Gwen said, returning the hug.

"Good morning, everyone." Kelly smiled.

"Good morning, Kelly," the room replied, at different tones and levels.

"Let's begin our meal," Kelly said.

Violet dipped her spoon into the bowl, and her taste buds lit up when the food touched her tongue. Vanilla! The smooth creaminess of the yogurt contrasted with the satisfying crunch of the granola, and she was overcome, ready to suck down the bowl, but she stayed in the moment and put the spoon down before taking another bite.

Kelly cleared her throat, which made everyone look up.

"All right, guys. Today is a special day for us all! Today is Violet's birthday!" Kelly clapped, and everyone followed suit. Violet worked to make her face look embarrassed, but she loved the attention.

"Thank you, everyone," she said, her cheeks burning in excitement.

"We all have birthdays, and we spend the day celebrating that we've been alive another year. Today Violet is twenty-one. She is getting older, as we all are. What does it mean to get older?" Kelly asked the group.

Gwen spoke up. "When I get older, I'm going to get married!"

"Gwen, let's stay in the present. We've discussed that before. We need to be in the here and now," Kelly said.

Gwen frowned. "But I've already started planning my wedding."

Kelly looked at Gwen. "What do you mean?"

"When I went to Target for personal needs shopping, I picked up a bridal magazine. I picked out my wedding dress and the dresses that I'll have my bridesmaids wear. In my sister's wedding, I wore a beautiful dress. It was like I was a princess, and I could hear the skirt crinkle when I spun around on the dance floor. I danced with my dad, and he told me that I *was* a princess." Gwen smiled at the memory.

"It's a lot of fun to dress up and go to parties," Kelly said. "I don't think that anyone would argue about that. As we all get older, the types of parties that we find fun change. When we were little kids, weddings may have seemed boring, but now they are exciting. That's a good example of getting older. Thank you, Gwen."

Across the table, Peter, another resident, giggled. Violet looked over to see what was so funny, and as soon as her attention was diverted to him, he said "Gwen, you are so *not* a princess!"

Gwen exploded on her other side. "Peter! You're such a damn idiot! You only laugh because you're jealous!" Gwen shouted across the table. Peter kept laughing, and when he saw that he'd made Gwen mad, he pointed and laughed, infuriating her further.

Violet stood up as Gwen did and put her hand on her friend's shoulder. "Gwen, Peter was mean for laughing at you, but getting mad at him back won't make it better. We're all friends here. You have to forgive him." Gwen gave Violet a hard look but sat back down, and Violet heard Peter laugh even harder. She turned to him. "Now, what's so funny, you big joker?"

Peter stopped laughing. Violet knew that she'd made him angry.

"Kelly," Peter started, "Last night I saw Violet eat her dinner way too fast."

"He's lying, Kelly. I did not," Violet protested. Now she was getting mad.

Kelly looked at Violet. "Vi, will you please sit down? Peter, we don't need to tattle on each other. We only need to tell someone if one of our friends is hurting themselves or someone else. If you were worried about Violet eating too fast last night, as her friend, you should have said something to her. This is a great opportunity to practice how we talk to our friends when we're concerned about them. Peter?"

Peter shook his head. He wasn't going to talk. Kelly looked at Violet. "Violet, would you show everyone how you would tell me if you thought I was eating too fast?" Kelly bent her head down over her cereal bowl and pretended to eat very quickly.

"Kelly, I'm your friend and I'm worried about you. I see that you're eating pretty fast, and I don't want you to choke." Violet was proud of herself for knowing how to use her words to voice a concern to her friend.

"Thank you for caring about me, Violet. I will try to slow down." Kelly looked up and smiled before turning her attention to the group again. "Does everyone have a better understanding of how we should talk to our friends?"

Everyone nodded, smiling. Violet beamed with satisfaction that she was the one who could offer that example to her housemates, and everyone was reminded of their good manners. "Well, ladies and gentlemen, it's off to work with you all." Kelly smiled at the group.

When Violet got home from work, she called her parents, just like she'd promised them that she would. Violet was almost overcome with joy when Lukas answered the phone.

"Luke!" she exclaimed. "Are you coming to visit me also?"

"It's my little sister's twenty-first birthday! Of course I'm coming to see you!" Lukas said, laughing. "I'm going to buy you a beer soon!"

"Lukas, I can't drink beer." Violet giggled.

"Well, better luck next time," Lukas said. "Here come Mom and Dad. I'm going to put you on speaker."

"Okay," Violet said, but before she could get the whole

word out, her family started singing "Happy birthday," and Violet was caught up in the excitement of their attention.

"Thank you!" Violet said, beaming.

"Are you having a good day, angel?" Ian asked.

"Yes!" Violet said. "I can't wait to see you this weekend!"

"We can't wait, either. We're so excited to see your game," Samantha said.

Violet smiled. "I love you all!"

That night, after basketball practice and a quick shower, Violet walked into the dining room for dinner and found the table covered in balloons and streamers.

"What's this?" she asked excitedly.

"It's your birthday party!" Kelly exclaimed. Everyone came forward to hug Violet, filling her with joy. They all took their seats, and then, as if on cue, started singing "Happy birthday."

Suzanne brought out a tray of two-bite brownies. Violet pretended to blow out a candle, and everyone laughed as Suzanne distributed the treats.

All the residents were excited to have kept a secret all day, and Violet soaked in the love, warmth, and security that came with firm boundaries and a sense of understanding about who she was beyond her Prader-Willi.

The next morning, Violet awoke more gradually than the day before. Although the day before had been her birthday and she was excited, this was different. Normally she woke up with her alarm clock, but today, she just wanted to roll over and go back to sleep.

"Violet, get up!" Stephanie called across the room.

"I am." Violet sat up and put her feet on the floor. She

collected her toiletries and trudged down the hall to the shower.

When she finally made it downstairs to breakfast, Violet just knew something was *off*. She was the last person to sit at the table, and when Suzanne put her bowl of oatmeal in front of her, Violet pushed it away and put her head on the table. Her belly hurt. She didn't want any breakfast.

"Hey, Vi." Kelly walked over to the girl and put her hand on Violet's shoulder.

"Hey," Violet said into her arm.

"Violet, could you look at me?" Kelly leaned down so that she was eye-to-eye with Violet.

Slowly raising her head, Violet locked eyes with her house manager. Kelly placed her hand on Violet's back. "You don't seem like yourself today," she said. "Are you sick, Violet?"

Violet shook her head. "I don't think so. I just want to go back to bed."

Kelly nodded and led Violet to her bed before calling the on-call nurse, who recommended that they go straight to the emergency room. Kelly left a quick message for Lauren so she could call Samantha and Ian and fill them in.

"Violet, we're going to have to go to the hospital," Kelly explained gently.

"I just want to rest," Violet protested.

"You can rest at the hospital," Kelly stood Violet up and helped her walk to the living room, where she waited for a staff member to take her to the hospital.

■ ■ ■

"Ian Durkin," Ian answered his ringing cell phone between clients.

"Hello, Mr. Durkin. This is Doctor Sawyer Hawes at Oconomowoc Hospital. As you know, Violet's staff brought her to the hospital this morning. They are still here with her, and I told them I would be happy to call and talk to you directly."

Ian's blood ran cold. "Yes? What's wrong with Violet?"

"She's currently resting. Violet refused her breakfast and complained of a stomachache this morning—which, of course, is unusual. She seemed fatigued, and staff described a general malaise. After a CT scan, we diagnosed her with an acute bowel obstruction. That's where feces become impacted in a section of the bowel and cannot move through."

"What?" Ian was horrified. Although he knew what a bowel obstruction was, he wasn't sure how severe his daughter's was.

"We need to perform a sigmoidoscopy in order to determine the location and severity of the obstruction. That requires anesthesia and your consent as her guardian. We've given her IVs to rehydrate her. We see patients from PWHO here often, and this is a common ailment. Because our patients with Prader-Willi have such high tolerances for pain, this ordeal, which can be life threatening, often seems anticlimactic. You're lucky to have her there, where they can recognize the symptoms and bring her in before it becomes a major problem," Dr. Hawes said.

"Of course, you have my consent. I live three hours away, but my wife and I will be there as quickly as we can." Ian rushed to hang up the phone, his adrenaline making his blood whoosh through his head.

Ian and Samantha saw Patty, a staff member at PWHO in the waiting room at the hospital. She rushed over when she saw them. "I came down so I could meet you when you arrived," Patty said.

"What's going on?" Ian asked.

"The doctors are waiting for you. They wouldn't tell me what's going on since you were on your way," Patty replied. Her concern for Violet was obvious. "She's on the fourth floor," Patty told them, as they all headed to the elevator together.

Upstairs, Ian asked about his daughter at the nurse's station and was directed to a doctor's office while Patty waited outside. Samantha shook her knees as she waited, her anxiety reaching a fever pitch. Why wouldn't anyone tell her what was going on? Why couldn't she see Violet?

"Mr. and Mrs. Durkin? I'm Dr. Hawes. I spoke to you on the phone, Mr. Durkin," a younger doctor, fresh out of residency, said as he walked into the office. His dark eyes shone above his caramel complexion. He ran his hand over his shaved head, as if he used to have hair and running his hands through it was a nervous habit.

"Yes. Nice to meet you Dr. Hawes. Where's our Violet?" Samantha asked, frantically.

"She's in recovery. We performed the sigmoidoscopy, which—"

"I am aware of what a sigmoidoscopy is," Ian interrupted. "I'm a doctor myself."

"Of course," Dr. Hawes said. "Well, we found the obstruction, and we immediately gave her antibiotics and fluids through an IV. We placed a nasogastric tube through her nose into her stomach to remove fluid and gas to relieve her pain and pressure. We then treated her with a liquid enema, which was successful in opening her blockage."

"Well, that's good news. When can we see her?" Samantha asked.

"She should be waking up anytime now, and we'd like to keep her alone in recovery for a few hours. You should be able to see her soon." Dr. Hawes replied.

"How did she develop a bowel obstruction of this nature so quickly?" Ian asked, perplexed. "It seems as though it would have been caught before it reached this critical point."

"Typically, the only symptoms that PW patients show are a general malaise and a lack of appetite. They usually don't complain about not feeling well, but Violet did say her stomach hurt. You or I would have been hospitalized a week ago, but again, since there are very few symptoms PW patients report, we're lucky that the staff at PWHO catches things as quickly as they do."

"Is there a reason *why* the bowl obstruction happened?" Samantha asked. "Is there a way to prevent it from happening again?"

"We think that because bowel obstructions so commonly occur in people with Prader-Willi," Dr. Hawes said, "it may have something to do with the hypotonia—the low muscle tone affects all the muscles, including the bowels. Since the intestines and colon are muscles that move things along, sometimes they get delayed. Also, the hypotonia makes it difficult to remove all the stool during a bowel movement, which can be a contributing factor."

"That makes sense," Samantha replied, nodding.

"If you don't have any other questions, feel free to sit in our family waiting room. We'll send out a nurse to get you when Violet is out of recovery." Dr. Hawes smiled and shook Ian and Samantha's hands while leading them into the hallway. They joined Patty in the waiting room and filled her in on what the doctor had told them. Then, they all waited.

Four hours later, Samantha had finished her novel and was vacantly watching the news the hospital had put on the television in the waiting room. She kept looking to the clock on the wall. They should have called them back to see Violet by now. The more she thought about it, the longer the minutes seemed to stretch. At last, the door opened, but instead of a nurse coming through, it was Dr. Hawes.

"Dr. and Mrs. Durkin," Dr. Hawes began, walking towards them. "I have some interesting news."

Samantha and Ian stood, their hearts pounding in anticipation.

"Violet came through everything just fine. Her vitals look good, but she is baffling us, as she still hasn't awakened from the anesthesia. Again, her systems are okay overall, but they're slowed down. We're moving her to ICU to keep monitoring her closely."

"Can we go see her?" Samantha asked, fat tears rolling down her cheeks. *What does he mean they can't wake her? ICU?*

"Certainly, but as she's still asleep, she is unresponsive." Dr. Hawes said, carefully. "To be perfectly honest, we've had every specialist in the hospital come to see her, and no one can find anything. It just seems like she's in a deep sleep."

. . .

The next morning, Samantha awoke with a stiff neck. She looked around and wondered how she got to a hospital room, the steady beep of the heart rate monitor keeping time. Then, she remembered her Violet—how she had gone under anesthesia and still hadn't woken. Samantha turned her head and saw Ian nodding in the other recliner the hospital had provided them. Patty had gone home but was scheduled to come back shortly. Samantha reached over and grabbed Violet's hands. Her daughter looked so fragile and sweet in her sleep, and Samantha hoped that she was having nice dreams.

"Violet, this is your mom," Samantha said softly. "You've been asleep for almost twenty-four hours. That's a whole day. We need you to wake up now."

Violet groaned and shifted.

"Violet?" Samantha stood and put her face close to her daughter's. "Violet! Can you hear me? Get up, sweetheart."

Violet stirred and her eyelids fluttered open. "Mom! What are you doing here?"

Samantha released a sob of relief. "Violet, you were very sick. The doctors had to look in your tummy and fix you. You're all better now, but we were worried about you."

Violet grinned at her mom. "I am all better now. And I got to see you. What a happy day this sickness brought!"

CHAPTER 18

On Wednesday afternoons, two of the houses at PWHO got together for a social. Violet was talking with Dane and Gwen when she realized that Gwen was looking behind her and not listening to what she was saying.

"Gwen!" Violet exclaimed. She hated when people didn't listen to her, but when Gwen still didn't respond, she turned around. Another house had gotten a new resident, and he walked into the social with his housemates. Violet heard everyone hustling to go talk to him, and when the crowd finally thinned enough for her to see through to the new boy, she could see what all the fuss was about—he was gorgeous. He was at least five four, taller than everyone else standing around him, with thick, strawberry blonde hair that was cut short in the back, but his bangs hung almost into his eyes. Violet's stomach fluttered, and she swallowed hard. She was in love.

"All right, gang," Michelle, a staff member from Violet's house, called out. "Let's all get together for our walk. I'm leading, and Nancy will be in the back. Paul, Devin, and Steve are going to be in the middle. Everyone needs to stay between us."

Violet coolly walked over to where everyone was gathered and just happened to stand next to the new guy.

"I'm Violet," she said, trying her best for a coy smile.

"Derek," he said, looking away as he blushed.

"I'm glad you live here. It's so much fun." Violet giggled. This was the first time she'd tried talking to a boy she liked. She wasn't sure how she was doing.

"Yeah. I think so," he said, more in grunts than words.

He must be shy, Violet thought. "Want to walk with me?" she asked him.

"Sure," he responded.

Violet linked her arm through his and started to walk towards the back of everyone else. "Where are you from?" she asked.

"Tennessee. I lived somewhere else like this before I lived here. It was bad. I hope this isn't bad." Derek finally looked up at her, and Violet saw his hazel eyes for the first time.

"It's really good!" she said. "You talk kind of funny. Is it because you're from Tennessee?"

"I guess so," Derek answered. He smiled. "I think you talk funny."

"No way!" Violet said. "Do you have a girlfriend?"

"Not anymore. I had one, but I had to leave her." Derek looked off.

"Do you miss her?" Violet asked, looking up at him again. He was wearing a blue flannel coat over his jeans. She could see an orange collar of a polo shirt poking out of the top. That prompted her to look down at her clothes—the grey pea coat that her mother bought her the last time she was home laid perfectly over her jeans. She'd lost so much weight in the years that she'd been at PWHO that shopping was a whole new experience for her. She was glad that she'd chosen that outfit for the social, as it was her favorite.

"I don't miss her so much anymore. Do you want to be my girlfriend?" Derek looked at her, his hazel eyes shining in the springtime sun.

"Since you don't live in my house, yes! I would love to be your girlfriend!" Violet tiptoed to kiss him on the cheek and he blushed again. She pulled her arm out from his, and he grabbed her hand. *A boyfriend!* she thought. *For me!* And he was so cute!

After their walk, she couldn't wait to tell Gwen and Stephanie that Derek was her boyfriend. When they got back to their house, Violet was bursting with the news.

"So, is Derek your boyfriend?" Gwen asked, before Violet could even say anything.

"Yes! How did you know?" Violet asked, disappointed that she couldn't say it first.

"You were holding hands with him. Duh!" Stephanie laughed.

"He's so cute!" Violet exclaimed.

"He is cute," Stephanie said. She used to have a boyfriend named Brian, but they had broken up. She had been sad when it ended.

"Vi, you ready?" Lauren's voice broke up the girl talk. It was time for Violet's private session with her, and in the excitement, Violet had almost forgotten.

"I'm coming, Lauren!" Violet hopped up off the couch to follow Lauren to her office.

"So, what's new with you, lady?" Lauren asked, after they were both seated.

"Derek is my boyfriend!" Violet almost squealed.

"Well, you seem happy, so that's wonderful. We'll have to tell your mom and dad this great news, and then we'll have to work on a dating contract, but let's have a conversation before we do that." Lauren smiled at Violet. Relationships weren't uncommon at PWHO, as people with Prader-Willi Syndrome were inclined to be affectionate. Everyone was different, but as this was the first time that Violet had been interested in a boy, Lauren knew that they needed to have a serious conversation about what it meant to have a boyfriend.

"I know. We're in love with each other. We'll probably get married," Violet gushed, a grin spreading over her face.

"It's a little soon to be talking about getting married, don't you think?" said Lauren, teasing Violet a little bit.

"You're right. Maybe we won't get married, but we'll be together forever." Violet said, reconsidering.

"What does that mean?" Lauren asked.

"It means that we're in love and he's the one. I saw that on TV. A girl was in love with her boyfriend and planned to kiss him after the prom," Violet recounted matter-of-factly.

"But what does kissing entail? It's a big deal. Are you sure you're ready for it?" Lauren leaned in, as though she was really interested in Violet's answer, and Violet wondered if Lauren had ever kissed a boy; she figured that she hadn't, and that's why she wanted Violet to tell her about it.

"It means that we'll put our mouths together and move them around," Violet explained carefully.

Lauren nodded and wrote something down. "Your relationship is still very new. Don't get in a big hurry to do anything just yet. You want to make sure that you know him very well before you decide you will be in love with him forever or say that he's the one. You just met him this afternoon. Be aware that sometimes relationships end."

"Like Stephanie and Brian?" Violet asked, her eyes wide.

"Just like that. It can be painful for you when you care about someone and you're not together anymore. Enjoy being with him, certainly, but just have fun with what you have right now," Lauren said.

"That makes sense, Lauren. Thank you." Violet smiled at her. She appreciated the guidance but wasn't sure that it was necessary. Derek loved her, too. They would be together forever.

• • •

Violet was sitting with Derek on the couch at his house on the fourth evening that they were dating. He reached over and put his arm around her, and she leaned in, relishing his closeness. She'd never been close like this with anyone but her family. No boy she went to high school with would have been interested in her like Derek was, and her heart pounded when he tilted his head and put his mouth to hers. She could taste the meatloaf that he'd had for dinner on his lips, and his skin was warm and scratchy from the little bit of patchy beard that hadn't been shaved that day. It was her first kiss, but she didn't want him to know that. She leaned in and kissed him harder.

"Derek and Violet, come on, guys. Kisses are wonderful, but let's separate a little," Patricia, a staff member at Derek's house, called out to them from the chair nearby. Violet pulled away, but Derek grabbed the back of her head and pressed his face to hers, continuing the kiss.

She put both of her hands on his chest and pushed away.

"Derek, Patricia asked us to stop. I don't want to get in trouble," Violet said to him when her face was finally free.

Derek growled, and Violet could see on his face that he was mad. He leaned backwards on the couch and started to bang his head on the wall.

"Derek, stop!" Violet shouted. She stood up and put her hands on his shoulders, trying to pull him from the wall, but he lifted both hands and shoved her off. She fell against the other wall, hitting her head on the baseboard. She was a little dizzy, but more than that, she was angry.

"Derek! I'm breaking up with you! I hate you and I never want to see you again!" Suddenly, Patricia was at Violet's side to make sure she was okay.

"What a bastard! He kept kissing me after you told us to stop. Then he pushed me. He's not a good boyfriend!" Violet told Patricia on their way back to her house.

"Are you okay, Violet?" Patricia asked. "Were you hurt?"

"I feel fine. I'm just mad," Violet replied.

At her house, Violet ran upstairs to her room. She flung herself into her bed, her body heaving with heavy sobs. Violet couldn't believe that he'd acted that way. He was supposed to be her boyfriend, the one who loves her, but he'd treated her like trash. Maybe she was trash and didn't deserve to be loved. Without meaning to, Violet started tugging at her hair as she wept, only stopping when a knock came at her door.

"Violet, can I come in?" Kelly's voice came through the room.

"Yes," Violet called, hoping her voice was loud enough for Kelly to hear her.

Kelly opened the door and sat in a chair at the foot

of Violet's bed. "Are you okay, Vi?" Her voice was sweet.

Violet shook her head. "My heart is broken."

Kelly wrapped her arms around Violet in a comforting hug. "We need to call your parents and tell them what happened. Do you want to come with me?"

Violet nodded, looking down.

"Wash your face and come down to my office. I'll have your parents on the line." Kelly stood up to go to the door. "The end of your first relationship is rough, Vi. Especially when it's like this and you didn't see it coming."

As Violet made her way into Kelly's office a few minutes later, she heard her house manager on the phone. "She's completely okay but really upset. Yes. Here she is now. I'll put you on speaker phone."

She clicked the phone over and motioned for Violet to have a seat.

"Hi, Mom." Violet's voice was small.

"Hey, Vi. Dad's here, too." When Violet heard her mother's voice, she wanted to wrap up in it like a blanket. "Heard you had a rough day."

"I did. I thought he loved me, and he hurt me." Violet's eyes filled up with tears as she spoke to her mother.

"This is one of the hardest parts about life. Boys will break your heart, and it has nothing to do with you," her mother reassured her.

"But Dad never broke your heart," Violet protested.

"No. He never did. But there were boys before your dad. When I was a little younger than you, I had a boyfriend who ended up taking another girl to his fraternity's dance instead of me. I was sad about that for months," her mother said.

"You had a boyfriend before Dad?" Violet asked. She

couldn't believe that her mom had ever kissed another boy.

"I didn't meet your dad until I was twenty-four. Yes, I had a boyfriend before him. And you know what, I'm glad it didn't work out with that guy. The last thing I heard about him was that he was raising snakes."

"Really? He raises snakes! What does he do with them then?" Violet giggled. The idea of her mother being married to someone who raised snakes was funny.

"I guess he sells them to his wife, Medusa, as hair. I don't know. What I'm saying is everything happens for a reason, Vi. You'll learn from this. Our only concern is that you're okay right now. You're not physically hurt?" Samantha's tone shifted back to a serious one.

"No. I'm all right. I promise." Violet looked around Kelly's office. Her mom's voice had been great, but she was anxious to get to dinner. Tonight the house was having spaghetti, and she was excited to have a piece of garlic bread. She wondered if she could use the breakup as an excuse to get dessert . . .

"We love you, Violet," said her dad, speaking up for the first time in the conversation.

"Love you too," Violet said, smiling a little. "Bye."

CHAPTER 19

"It's Christmas, everyone!" Violet cried, running down the hallway at her parents' house and knocking on everyone's bedroom door. "Wake up! We have to open presents!"

She ran down the stairs, where her dad left the Christmas tree lit the night before so she could see her way around the living room. There were tons of presents under the tree! The stockings were stuffed with goodies, and Violet wanted to open all of the gifts as fast as she could. Instead, she did a little dance in her bare feet around the tree, waiting for everyone to come downstairs. It didn't take them long. Her parents were laughing, along with Lukas, who'd come home from UCLA, where he'd just finished his Ph.D., and Mitchell with his wife, Angie.

"There are presents!" Violet exclaimed. "What are we waiting for, people?" The family chuckled again, but Violet couldn't understand why they were all taking the situation so lightly. "This is serious!"

There was a strained pause before Ian ushered them all to the gifts, and the next twenty minutes were spent ripping into wrapping paper and sparkling bags.

"Breakfast, guys," Ian called out after all the presents were open. Violet sat at the dining table, and Samantha made her a plate of pancakes and sausage. Mitchell's wife, Angie, sat next to Violet, and to distract herself from eating before everyone else, Violet reached over and rubbed Angie's belly. She was six months pregnant, and Violet couldn't wait to be Auntie Vi in March.

"You made a baby with Mitchell, didn't you?" Violet asked her, still rubbing her sister-in-law's belly.

Angie looked embarrassed and glanced around at her in-laws. Violet wasn't sure why. She figured that there was a baby in her belly, and Angie was his wife, and that was okay. Lukas wasn't married yet, though. Maybe no one had told him how that worked. Maybe that's why Angie was embarrassed; Violet wasn't supposed to tell him.

Instead, she said, "Angie, I can't wait to be an auntie!"

Angie smiled. "Thank you for that, Violet."

"Vi, that's a very personal conversation. Those aren't best had at the breakfast table." Samantha looked over at her daughter from across the table.

"Mom, Lauren talks to me about circles. We all have circles. The closest circle to you is your family, and you don't have any secrets. You can talk about anything with your family. The next circle includes your close friends, and they are a little farther away, so you can have some secrets from them. The next circle is for strangers, and we don't share personal things with them. Angie is married to Mitchell now, and that means she's family, too. We're just having girl talk." Violet was proud to present her reasoning to her mother.

"Let's save the girl talk until it's just you girls," Ian said from the head of the table. He winked at his daughter to indicate that he wasn't mad, but he was serious.

Violet nodded, feeling awkward. "Sorry," she muttered to Angie, who smiled and wrapped her arm around Violet, making her feel better immediately.

A couple of hours later, the house was still as everyone slept off breakfast, except Violet, who was sitting on the couch. She was watching *Rudolph the Red Nosed Reindeer*, but she was bored, and her stomach gnawed angrily.

Just to see what was in there, she snuck into the kitchen. Then her eyes widened: her dad must be out of practice. He'd left the keys in the pantry door. Instantly, Violet raced toward it, letting herself inside and closing the door behind her. The pantry was dark and warm, and Violet sank to the floor with the first box her hands landed on: honey buns. In no time, twelve wrappers fell to the floor around her with a satisfying crinkle. The next closest thing to her was a bag of crunchy oatmeal cookies. Her mouth was full, and she had her hand in the bag for another when Mitchell opened the pantry door, catching her red-handed.

"Violet, what the hell are you doing?" he exclaimed, rushing towards his sister. He ripped the bag of cookies from her, but she still had a fistful and she shoved them in her mouth. The new cookies pushed the chewed up cookies to the back of her throat. She tried to breath, but there was nowhere for the air to go. Her eyes widened as she began to choke.

"Dad! Get in here! Now!" Mitchell yelled. He turned Violet around and positioned his hands beneath her sternum.

"Move, Mitch!" Violet's father pushed past Mitchell, and she wasn't sure what to make of it when he wrapped his arms around her and ran his closed fists up against her stomach, hard. "Violet, I know that this is uncomfortable, but I'm getting the . . ."

Violet coughed, and the cookies all flew out of her mouth and onto the floor. She pulled in one desperate gasp of air before squatting down, her eyes feral as she collected the gooey mess and pushed it back into her mouth.

"What just happened?" Ian asked his son, frantically.

"I just came in here to get some water for Angie. Violet was in the pantry. Obviously, she'd already gotten to the honey buns, and she was working on those cookies. I tried to get them from her . . ." Mitchell was still overwhelmed by what had just happened.

"You should know better than to try to get food from her!" Ian said angrily. "What the hell were you thinking?"

"What the hell was I thinking? You're right. I don't know what I was thinking turning down a cruise to Aruba with my pregnant wife and my in-laws to be here in this snowy hell with a family that has never appreciated me. I really thought that this strained relationship might be my fault. And since I'm having a son, I wanted to atone for all the Christmases that I'd missed by choice. But it turns out that I was wrong. Have your happy crappy Christmas with the children who make you proud, Dr. Durkin. I'm done with this shit." Mitchell's face was red, contrasting with his fair hair. He turned on his heel and stomped upstairs.

Ian fell to his knees, consumed with guilt for the way he'd handled himself in his tenuous relationship with his son and for the fact that he was the one who'd left the pantry keys accessible to Violet, even if it was accidental. He didn't even have the energy to stop Violet when she reached for a package of granola bars.

A few hours later, the Durkin family sat down to a silent Christmas dinner. Mitchell and Angie had left just after the fight, Samantha and Ian pushed their food around their plates, and nobody seemed sure what to say to anyone else. Violet was uncomfortable, too, and felt bad for the trouble she'd caused, but at the same time, all afternoon she'd thought of those moments alone in the pantry, reliving the joy of being able to grab whatever she wanted, totally unsupervised. Now, though, she felt a need to break the tension.

"Come on, Luke." Violet smiled at her brother. "Let's sing Jingle Bells."

"What?" he asked.

"You know the words. Jingle bells, jingle bells . . ." Violet started. When no one joined in with her, she grew quiet again.

"Jingle all the way . . ." Luke winked at his sister, singing in a funny voice.

"Oh, what fun it is to ride, in a one-horse open sleigh . . ." The whole family joined on that line, everyone using the same funny voice as Lukas even if no one quite met anyone else's eyes.

CHAPTER 20

Violet awoke to her dark, still room. She glanced around, seeing that her alarm clock read five ten; she still had twenty minutes until she had to wake up. Something was different about the day, and after trying to make out the corners of her room in the dark, she remembered what it was.

"Today is my birthday," Violet said to her roommate, Charlotte. Stephanie had moved into a different house the year before—she was too old to keep up with the stairs where she used to live. "Today I'm forty, Charlotte."

Charlotte rolled over grumpily. "Well, that means you're a grown up."

Violet giggled a bit at Charlotte's response but rolled out of bed, deciding to let the alarm clock wake Charlotte in twenty minutes. Violet rushed to the bathroom with her personal supplies, and after the shower, took note of the grey hair building along her hairline. She frowned at her reflection—her mother didn't have grey hair until she was much older than forty. Only recently had Samantha's hair started to grey, and for a moment, Violet was relieved that her mother had gotten too old to color her hair any longer—Violet couldn't look older than the woman who had given birth to her. Violet thought about Stephanie and how her hair was completely grey now. When Stephanie moved out, Kelly explained to Violet that people with Prader-Willi used to only live to be twenty years old, but now they were living a lot longer. As a result, everyone was learning as they went about how to keep taking care of people with the syndrome when they got older. The best solution that PWHO had found was to open a new home designed just for the people who were not able to do the stairs anymore or who needed more help as they got older. Stephanie had to use a walker because she had osteoporosis, which meant that her bones weren't as strong as they used to be.

Violet walked down the stairs and into the kitchen, only to find that she was the only person in the house ready for the day. Kelly was sitting on the couch with her computer, and when she saw Violet, she smiled and rose to give her a hug.

"Happy birthday, Violet," she said. "How are you feeling?"

"I'm good, how are you?" Violet returned the hug and smile. She loved feeling special on her birthday.

"I'm good too, thanks. Getting ready to work with Alicia today. You understand that you're going to be working with her more now, right?" Kelly's eyebrows rose just slightly with her question.

Violet nodded. While she'd worked with Kelly for twenty-one years, she understood that Kelly was going through a process of retirement. That meant Alicia would take over as her house manager eventually, but for now, they both worked there some.

"Don't forget that your family wants to video chat with you today," Kelly said, smiling.

"I won't! That will be so much fun!" Violet was excited to see her family. Since her parents were getting older, they didn't get to visit every weekend anymore. Once a month, Lukas and his wife, Emily, came to take Violet to see her parents. She was thrilled to be able to see them today, even if it was on a screen.

That afternoon after work, Violet dialed her brother Lukas's video account. He picked it up after two rings, and she saw her parents sitting on the couch holding balloons.

"Happy birthday, Violet!" everyone called out in unison.

"Did you get our package?" Samantha asked first. Her face had started to look like a crinkly piece of paper, and her hair was completely grey, but she still had her beauty. The only difference that Violet noticed between now and the last time she'd seen her mother was that her mother's eyes weren't as blazingly blue as usually were.

"Yes! I love the raspberry lotion!" Violet cried out. "You also got me some great movies that I will have fun watching with my new roommate, Charlotte. She's never seen any good romantic comedies, because she's so young. We'll fix that today!"

Emily giggled. "You set her straight, Vi!"

"I know! Thank you all for calling me. I love and miss you all, and I will see you next month." Violet blew kisses at the screen. Her attention had started to wander, and cutting the call short was the nicest thing to do. Samantha reached out and touched the screen. Violet watched as her mother's hand got bigger than her face.

"I love you so much, my sweet Violet," Samantha said, with tears in her eyes.

"I love you too, Mom. I'll see you soon, everyone!" Violet

ended the call, happy to have talked to her family but ready for her birthday surprise. Because it was her birthday, she got to pick the afternoon activity. She chose a little game of basketball between the houses, since she was too old to play for the Special Olympics anymore and missed it. Everyone gathered at the basketball court outside where she'd played as a young woman, and when she got the ball, the excitement coursed through her just as it had years ago.

Violet held the ball in position, jumping to take the shot. She heard the ball *swoosh* through the net and ran back across the court to get ready for the next play. But her feet must have been going faster than her brain, because she slipped and ended up on the cement. Looking down, she saw that her ankle was bent at a peculiar angle.

Alicia rushed over to her. "Oh, God, Violet. I think it's broken," she said, before she called out for an ambulance. Violet didn't remember anything else until she woke up in a hospital bed. She pressed the nurse's button since she had no idea what was going on.

A petite woman who looked like she was about twenty-five came to her bed. "Yes, Violet. You're awake!"

"What happened?" Violet asked groggily.

"You came in last night. You were talking, but everyone knew that you weren't lucid because what you were saying didn't make any sense. The doctors did an x-ray of your leg, and your anklebone was broken in half diagonally. The bone broke in such a way that it cut into your muscle, and we had to do surgery last night. We had to put in a metal rod so that you would heal properly. Violet," the nurse asked slowly, "did you know that you had osteoporosis?"

"I don't have that. Stephanie has that. I drink my milk every day," Violet countered. She couldn't believe that the nurse was telling her this. It just wasn't true.

The nurse smiled at her. "I believe you. Do you need anything at all, maybe some breakfast?"

Violet's eyes lit up. The nurse must not know about Prader-Willi! Having lived at PWHO for so long, Violet forgot that so many people in the rest of the world didn't know what Prader-Willi was, so they didn't keep things locked or stick to a schedule. "Yes," Violet said politely. "That would be great."

The nurse handed her a menu from the hospital cafeteria. "You order whatever you want. You've had a rough day, and it was your birthday, right?"

"It was my birthday." Violet gave the nurse her best sad face. "Did you say I could order whatever I wanted?"

"You do whatever you need to do. Here's the phone so you can call the cafeteria. Dawn, your staff member, just took a break to go to the bathroom. She'll be right back." The nurse smiled at Violet and walked away, completely clueless to the Pandora's box she'd just opened.

Without wasting any time, Violet picked up the phone and ordered breakfast. She hadn't had this kind of freedom in twenty years, and she planned to take advantage of it.

"Yes, ma'am, I need an order of pancakes and sausage, a bowl of oatmeal, a three-egg omelet with cheddar cheese, an extra side of turkey bacon, and . . . fruit salad," Violet said into the phone.

"That sure is a lot of breakfast," the cafeteria worker remarked.

"I'm a hungry girl," Violet replied. Then, remembering

her manners, she added, "Thank you." She hung up the phone.

Fifteen minutes later, she had a tray with pancakes and sausage, oatmeal, and an omelet spread before her.

"Violet, did you order all this food?" the nurse asked, walking back in.

Violet gave the nurse a dirty look as she shoved pancakes into her mouth. "Yes, but they're still bringing me more," she managed, working her tongue around the soft dough.

"I think you have plenty of food right here," the nurse said with a smile. "We don't want you to get sick. I'm going to cancel the rest of your order. You'll be fine with this." The nurse's voice was sweet, but all Violet could hear was no. Her leg was in traction, so she couldn't move much. All she knew was that this woman was *not* going to take her food away.

"No!" Violet cried. She thought quickly, trying desperately not to grab at the rest of her food. "Listen. You don't understand. I haven't had anything to eat in . . . days. Four days. Maybe a week."

The nurse paused with her hand over the phone. Her eyebrows furrowed. "Violet, are you telling me the truth now?"

"Yes!" Violet said, and while the nurse seemed to consider, she crammed three pieces of sausage into her mouth. She nodded fervently, feeling slightly guilty that she might get PWHO in trouble, but the hospital would find out soon enough that Violet was lying; no harm, no foul.

"Okay, well, that seems like a conversation we should have when your staff member comes back," the nurse said. "For now I'm just going to—" The nurse reached into Violet's bed and retrieved the phone.

Violet cried out, "No!" and reached up to knock the phone from the nurse's hand.

Shocked, the nurse stumbled forward, bumping into Violet's bed and knocking her leg out of traction.

"Dammit!" Violet howled. Almost reflexively, she pulled her right fist back and punched the nurse right in the jaw. *There. That should do it,* Violet thought, expecting the nurse to just fall over in a peaceful-looking sleep the way it happened in the movies.

"I can't believe you just did that!" the nurse cried, touching her jaw. Her eyes were round and angry. "You *assaulted* me. I'm calling security!" She ran out of the room, closing the door behind her. Violet vaguely heard a commotion in the hallway but only gathered her plate onto her lap and continued eating, hoping that the cafeteria workers would still bring her a second course.

As Violet greedily spooned the last of her oatmeal into her mouth, the door to her room opened. She smiled in anticipation of the worker who'd brought her the first course, but instead it was Dawn, the staff member from PWHO. She frowned as she walked toward Violet's hospital bed.

"I was only gone for fifteen minutes to stretch and go to the bathroom! I thought you'd sleep through it," Dawn said, shaking her head. "What's going on here, Vi?"

"I was just trying to order breakfast when that bitch nurse decided to cancel my food. Dawn, I've been in the hospital now for a long time. I needed to eat something. I haven't had anything since lunch yesterday, and God only knows when they'd feed me again!" Violet protested.

"Violet, you can't punch a nurse. Besides, look at all these empty plates and bowls. Looks to me like you've already had breakfast and then some," Dawn said, motioning with her hand at the accumulation on the table.

Violet looked down. She was caught in a lie.

"What's going to happen?" Violet asked, no longer angry but anxious about what would happen next.

"Nothing. She called security, but we were able to explain everything to them, and they aren't calling the police or pressing charges, thankfully. What we have to do is get you stabilized and home as quickly as possible." Dawn shook her head again. "Violet, would you like to apologize? I think you'd feel better if you do."

Violet knew that Dawn was right and nodded her head. "I know. And I will. Just as soon as I get a nap."

CHAPTER 21

"Whatever you're feeling right now is perfectly normal," Dean Kaplan, the minister and social worker that hospice had assigned to the Durkin family, told Lukas and Mitchell. "I understand that your mother has lived a very full life, and I think that understanding end of life care as a part of that process, rather than something to be overcome, will prove helpful in dealing with your reactions."

The man, who was a few years younger than Mitchell at forty-two, leaned forward on Samantha and Ian's couch. Mitchell ran his hand through his recently thinning hair. He couldn't anticipate his reaction to this, and he was angry that a stranger was in his parents' house trying to *tell* him how to deal with it. He could feel his chest puffing up, a typical Mitchell reaction to everything, when Lukas spoke to break the building tension.

"Thank you so much. My brother and I are different people, but at least we get to make our peace with Mom. This time is a blessing, and we're trying to deal with it as such." Lukas made himself smile. He'd inherited his father's sensibility in dealing with people. "This just all happened so quickly. Mom goes to the doctor a week ago because her back hurt and comes home with a diagnosis that she has pancreatic cancer and it's already spread up her spine and is headed to her brain." He shook his head, still in disbelief at his own words. "I think that we're still trying to make sense of the whole thing. I can assure you that we'll call you if we need any help." Lukas stood, indicating to the minister that the conversation was over.

"Would you like for me to pray with your mother before I go?" Dean asked, gathering his bag.

"I think you should pray *for* her. And us, thanks." Lukas showed the man to the door and came back in to take a seat with his brother. He caught a glimpse of himself in the decorative mirror hung over the couch. Long gone was the joke that he was starting to resemble Wolverine from X-Men; his face hadn't seen a razor in a week now, and he looked more like a lumberjack. He ran his hand through his still thick, but now more-salt-than-pepper hair, and for a moment could have sworn he saw his dad in the mirror. Their resemblance had always been uncanny, but the older he got, the stronger it became. He looked over at his brother on the couch. His polar opposite in every way, Mitchell was a smaller man with dirty blond hair that still wasn't graying. His hazel eyes looked tired and dull in his fair complexion. Although it had been at least as long since Mitchell had shaved, he had little more than a five o'clock shadow. The scientist and the artist, who shared more genetics with each other than anyone else, were face to face with each other and a crisis.

"What about Violet?" Mitchell asked. "I keep thinking about her. Our lives have completely stopped, and she's still in Wisconsin with no idea."

"And we should keep things this way," Lukas said. "I talked with Lauren when this all started. She strongly urged us not to tell Violet about this ahead of time, but to let her process it with us when she comes home. And can you imagine having her here now? She wouldn't understand what was going on."

"It's not fair to leave her in the dark, Luke. She and Mom need to have their time. They should be able to say their goodbyes. Violet should have the same opportunity that we've been given. You just said yourself that this was a blessing. How could you possibly deny her that?" Mitchell shot back, his eyes narrowing.

"Mitchell, what are we supposed to do? I was just as torn as you are until I talked to Lauren. She knows Violet. She knows her condition. She knows what is best, Mitch. Mom wouldn't want Violet to see her like this. She doesn't even know who we are anymore. Mom called her after she was diagnosed, and could still talk a few weeks ago. Dad's been calling Vi each week. She got to talk to Violet. We'll deal with this when we have to," Lukas reasoned.

"Lukas, you're only thinking about yourself!" Mitchell's voice was rising.

"No, Mitch, that's you. Who's going to take care of her? Make sure that her schedule is kept intact? We can't commit to that right now, and Violet will fall apart." Lukas was starting to lose his cool, a reaction that only his brother could provoke from him. He opened his mouth to continue, sitting up straighter on the couch, when he heard his father enter the room.

"Boys, I think you both should come in now," Ian said quietly. He was approaching his eightieth birthday, and while he was in great health physically, the prospect of losing his partner had broken him emotionally. He hadn't left her side for the six days that hospice care had been set up, his sons had made him eat, and he'd only catnapped in the recliner that he'd set up next to her hospital bed. He was relieved when both of his sons had come as soon as they could.

Lukas and his wife Emily had moved back to Lukas's hometown from LA last year, when they found out, officially, that they couldn't have children. Lukas left his tenured position at UCLA for a research job at a local, smaller university so that Emily could pursue a tenure-tracked job at another local college. Mitchell and Angie had never left the suburbs, but Mitch's job as an art teacher at a private high school could be demanding, and with three kids to support, he was always reluctant to take time off work. Despite the differences Ian and Samantha had had with their sons over the years, Ian was still proud that they were there for each other when it mattered.

The three men walked into Samantha's bedroom silently. A few minutes earlier, Ian had been sitting quietly by his wife's side. The cancer had spread so quickly that she'd been comatose for the past forty-eight hours. He knew that it wouldn't be long until he had to say his final goodbye. Suddenly, her body lurched up, and her breathing became even shallower than it had been. As a doctor, he knew what this meant, but he looked over at Rita, the hospice nurse assigned to the family. She nodded at him. "I'll give you some space," she said quietly, leaving the room and closing the door softly behind her.

Ian resumed his seat in the recliner and took his wife's hand. Mitchell stayed by the doorway, his eyes focused on the floor just next to his mother's bed. His eyes filled with tears, and he could do nothing but watch, silently, as Lukas walked over to his mother's feet. As an anthropologist who only knew of spiritual rituals that he'd studied from other cultures, all Lukas could think to do was rub his mother's legs, down to her feet, as hard as he could. He'd studied a small tribe of people in Central America who did that for their dying. They thought that the spirit needed help moving out of the body and that if someone the person loved helped it along, the spirit would know it was okay to leave. Lukas had found this quaint at the time, but now that he was in the same room as death, he wondered if there was some truth to it. Lukas closed his eyes and felt an electricity of sorts move through his arms. When he opened his eyes, he saw that his father had lowered his face to Samantha's hand that he was still holding. He kissed her fingers. "Sweet dreams, my love," he said. His voice was surprisingly clear.

Behind Lukas, Mitchell collapsed. Loud sobs escaped him. Ian got up, and despite the arthritis in both of his knees, knelt beside his son, collecting his head into his lap and smoothing his blonde hair. "She loved you, Mitch. She loved you so much," he whispered to him, almost rocking him.

Lukas didn't know what to do. He squeezed his mother's foot, where his hand was still resting. "Until we meet again," he whispered, making his way around his brother and father and out of the room.

Rita read the look on his face immediately. "I'm so sorry for your loss," she said, putting a hand to his shoulder. "I'll call the doctor to pronounce the time of death. Do you need to make arrangements?"

Lukas shook his head. "Mom was a planner. This was

all taken care of years ago. I just need to make a few phone calls."

Lukas first called his wife, Emily. Since end-of-life care was tricky, Lukas had insisted that she go to work that day. No one could predict exactly when his mother would go, and he wanted Emily to have more flexibility when it came to making arrangements for Violet rather than use up her time before Samantha passed. Emily offered to leave work immediately, but Lukas told her that she'd need the rest of the week off. He needed her to drive to Wisconsin with him to break the news to Violet.

After contacting the funeral home and the insurance company, Lukas made the call that he'd most dreaded. He crossed his fingers that Lauren would be at Violet's home this morning. While Alicia was fantastic, he wanted someone who had known Violet all these years to be the one who was with him when he broke this news to her the next morning.

"Hello," Lauren answered the phone on the second ring.

"Oh, thank God you're there." Lukas seemed to exhale the words.

"Is this Luke?" Lauren asked.

"Yes. Mom's gone. It just happened, not even an hour ago," Lukas said. He'd been able to make the professional arrangements and tell his wife, but somehow telling Lauren was different. His voice broke as he continued, "Emily and I will be there to get Violet first thing in the morning. I'd like to get there before she goes to work but after breakfast so we don't have that concern on the drive back. What time would be best?"

"Be here at seven thirty," Lauren said. "Wait in my office. I'll bring her in there around seven forty-five, and we can all tell her together. Before you come, let's talk this out. We have to decide on an approach with Violet that will minimize her anxiety and allow her to better understand what's going on."

"Okay," Lukas said, thankful that Lauren's head was clearer than his was. "What do you think will be best?"

"I'll pull her into the office. She'll be excited but confused because it will deviate from her schedule, and then she'll see you and Emily. I think that we should sit her down and tell her that your mother is gone. We'll normalize anything that she feels and allow her to ask questions. Any questions that you can't field or answer, I'll take care of," Lauren said, reassuringly. "Lukas, I really am so sorry for your loss. Samantha was a wonderful woman. She will be greatly missed."

Lukas wiped his eyes. "She certainly will. Thank you for everything, Lauren. I'll see you in the morning. Please don't mention anything to Violet yet. Are you still sure that's the right thing to do?" Suddenly, Lukas was questioning himself and the advice that Lauren had offered him the week before.

"Yes, Luke. We don't want Violet to have time to fall into her anxiety or to obsess about this prior to your coming. That can lead to an acute psychiatric decomposition at these times. Normally, we want to give our Prader-Willi clients lots of notice for something as simple as a change in a mealtime, but we don't want her to crash emotionally. With these kinds of situations and the emotional trauma involved, less foreshadowing is a better approach. When you get here, the business of packing her clothes, traveling, and then the wake and funeral will keep her centered and in place emotionally. A lot of times with these situations, we can expect the grief to hit her later, much later, than it will hit everyone else." Lauren took a deep breath. "I'm hurting for you all, and if there's anything else that you need, just give me a call."

"I will. Thanks, Lauren."

"Goodbye, Luke."

"Goodbye." He ended the call on his cell phone and looked around. He hadn't even realized that he'd walked out onto the patio in his parents' backyard. This backyard had been his haven when he was a kid, and now it was the place where he was first mourning the loss of his mother.

The next morning, Lukas and Emily pulled their sedan into the driveway at Violet's house, and Emily looked at her husband.

"You doing okay? You've been surprisingly cool about all of this." She reached over and put her hand on his shoulder.

"Yeah. I mean, I'm as okay as I can be. I'm really trying to hold myself together for Violet right now. She will feed on my emotion. Once there are more people around for her, I'll do my grieving thing. I promise, doctor." He half-smiled at his joke. "I'm glad you're here, Em. Violet loves you."

"And I love her. I feel like she's mine, just like you are." Emily smiled at Lukas, looking into his bottomless brown eyes. Unable to have children of her own, Emily had adopted Violet into her heart the day she met her, even though Violet was almost ten years her senior. Now she'd agreed, along with Lukas, to take legal guardianship of her. Emily looked at the clock on the dashboard; it read seven twenty-eight. "We need to get inside."

"You're right." Lukas unbuckled his seatbelt and moved to open the door. He began his long, sad walk to the side door that Lauren left unlocked so that he and Emily could get into her office without Violet seeing them.

In the next room, Lauren was talking to the residents as Kelly was wrapping up breakfast. As everyone started to disperse, Lauren called out to Violet.

"Hey, Vi, can I talk to you in my office for a few minutes?"

"What? I have to go to work," Violet said, feeling a small measure of distress. "I can't be late. Timeliness is very important, Lauren. You taught me that."

"Don't worry about that today. We have something to talk about." Lauren put her hand in the crook of Violet's arm and led her to the office door.

"Lauren, this isn't our time to meet! This is time for me to go work!" Violet cried, pushing Lauren's hand off her arm.

"Violet, please come with me," Lauren said quietly. Her tone indicated to Violet that this was serious, and she allowed herself to be led into Lauren's office.

"Luke! Emily!" Violet exclaimed. "It's a special surprise! That's why Lauren wanted me to come in here! How exciting!" Violet walked over to her brother and sister-in-law, who were sitting on the leather couch against the wall opposite the door.

"Hey, Vi." Emily stood and embraced her sister-in-law. "It's good to see you. Will you sit down with us so that we can talk for a minute?"

"Sure," Violet said, taking a seat in one of the two chairs adjacent to the couch. "What's going on? Am I going home?"

Lukas looked up at Lauren, who nodded to indicate he

should take the lead in this conversation.

"Violet, you are coming home. Mom passed away yesterday. You're coming home to be with us as we lay her to rest." Lukas looked at his sister, not sure what kind of sense she would make of this. He had prepared himself for this, but in the moment, he realized that there was no preparation for telling your little sister that her mother was no longer alive.

Violet paused, looking between Lukas, Emily, and Lauren. Luke's words seemed to float in the air before coming to settle at her feet. "She . . . died?" Violet asked uncertainly.

"Yes," Lukas responded quietly.

"Are you sad, Luke?" Violet tilted her head towards him.

"I am, Vi." Lukas shifted in his seat, meeting his sister's green-eyed gaze. Her almond-shaped eyes searched his, and he let her look.

"Vi, do you have any questions?" Lauren asked gently, breaking the stare between brother and sister.

"No," Violet said softly. Then: "Wait. Is Dad dead, too?"

"No, sweetie. Your dad is still at home," Lauren said. "You're going to see him this afternoon. Your family is all going to be very sad when you get home, just like Lukas is sad. It's okay if you're sad, too."

Violet considered that point for a moment before asking Lauren, "Is it okay if I cry at home?"

"Yes. It is perfectly okay if you feel like you need to cry. You can have any reaction that you feel, as long as you don't hurt yourself or anyone else. Remember how we talked about paying attention to those emotions that could be harmful?"

"Yes. I remember. I need to pack my clothes if I'm going home," Violet said. "Luke and Emily, do you promise you'll wait for me?"

"Of course, we will, Vi. Do you need any help?" Emily asked her.

"Yes. I want you to meet everyone. They haven't met my favorite little sister yet." Violet smiled and took Emily's hand, leading her out of the room.

CHAPTER 22

"Violet, sweetie, it's six thirty. Time for you to get up." Alicia's voice rang through Violet's bedroom, but Violet still laid under the covers. Her open eyes didn't even move in Alicia's direction. For three weeks, Violet hadn't been to work, hadn't done anything except shower and come down to the table for meals. Alicia had been patient, explaining to Violet that it was normal to feel sad, even though her mother had died nine months ago. When Violet returned from Samantha's funeral, she had gained fifteen pounds, and the next week, the house had a party to celebrate Kelly's official retirement. Violet's whole world changed in a matter of two weeks, and she had rainclouds in her head and her heart. Violet finally realized exactly how unfair life could be, and she wanted everyone to leave her alone.

"Violet." Alicia moved towards her, and Violet heard the chair at the foot of her bed squeak with Alicia's weight. "I'm worried about you. You won't come down except for mealtimes, and I miss our talks. Do you think we could talk now?"

Violet shook her head and pulled up the covers. She didn't want to talk to her. She wanted to talk to Kelly. She wanted to talk to Lauren. She wanted to talk to her mom.

They knew her a long time before Alicia was even born. Alicia was only thirty. Violet was forty-one. That meant she was eleven years old when Alicia was born. Alicia had the long, blonde curly hair that Violet had always wanted when she was younger. The first time that Violet met her, she asked Alicia if she'd ever seen a show that Violet used to watch when she was a teenager, and Alicia said it was before her time. Violet wondered if the house manager knew that after she was born, nothing else was ever cool again.

"So, Violet," Alicia continued, "I talked with Kelly."

Violet popped her head out of the quilt. Alicia had gotten her attention.

"And she was telling me how much you love to get pedicures. So, I was thinking that might be a fun thing for us to do together," Alicia continued.

"Really?" Violet asked.

"Yep. But, the problem is I only have enough money for one pedicure, and if you don't start going to work, we can't go together. How do you think we can solve that?" Alicia asked, cocking her head to the side.

Violet shook her head. "I don't know."

Alicia nodded sympathetically. "I understand. What could we do to motivate you to go to work so that we can have our pedicure?"

Violet shook her head again. All was lost if she couldn't get a pedicure when one was offered.

"What if, every morning that you get up on time, perform all of your hygiene, your morning chores, and go to work, you'll get three tickets? Once you have twenty tickets, we can trade them in for a movie. If you're able to save up to fifty tickets, we can get a pedicure together." Alicia paused. She wanted to use collaborative problem solving with Violet, but the girl was so deep in her mourning that she couldn't come up with any ideas.

Violet thought about the proposition for a moment. "Okay, Alicia. I'll do it. Can we start today?"

"We sure can. But you'd better hurry. Breakfast starts in thirty minutes, and you have a lot to get done." Alicia smiled. "Tell you what, I'll even give you a signing bonus: because you've agreed to our new system, this afternoon you and I will have some time to chat together outside, at the park."

"Really?" Violet jumped out of bed. While the rainclouds were still heavy on her chest, the idea that Alicia really wanted to spend time with her made her feel better. Violet thought about it in the shower. She really missed her mom and Kelly. Mom was never going to come back because she'd died. Violet hadn't gone home in three months because her dad had been selling the house and moving in with Lukas and Emily. Violet planned to go home the following weekend, but she knew that she would never return to the house that had been her home all of her life. Luke explained that another family lived in it now. Violet knew that things would be different, and more than anything, she just felt lonely. Going back to work and then having coffee with Alicia would be nice, she decided, and a smile played at the corners of her mouth.

It was nice weather that afternoon, so Alicia and Violet settled themselves on a bench, enjoying the sunshine on their shoulders.

"Oh! I don't want to forget," Alicia said, handing over three purple tickets to Violet. They were about the size of Violet's palm. "They're purple because they belong to you, Violet." She smiled.

Violet looked at the tickets. Pride shone in her eyes. "Thank you," she said.

"Are you missing your mom, Violet?" Alicia asked, putting a gentle hand on Violet's forearm.

Violet looked down. "Yeah. I am. I'm supposed to go home this weekend, and I don't know what to expect. I wonder if Luke and Emily are going to have the cabinets secured like I need. I wonder if they're going to keep my schedule the same. I know that some things will be different, because they have to be. I'm on a visit. But I wonder if they will keep me safe—like Mom always did."

"I think that your concerns are very valid, Violet. I'm pleased that you're talking about them with me. What do you think that we can do to ease your anxiety about this visit?" Alicia asked, pulling out a yellow pad of paper and a pen.

"I think we can give Emily and Luke a copy of my schedule. It would make me feel better if it was hanging somewhere where we could all see it. Then they would know what we should be doing."

Alicia made a note. "We can definitely do that. We can type it all out, and I can even email it over to them so that they have it today. It's only Wednesday, so they will have lots of time to prepare that way. What else can we do?"

"Could we ask them if they would tell me what we're going to eat and when? I'd like to know that food is coming," Violet suggested. She always felt better when she knew when her next meal would be. She felt even better when I knew *what* it would be.

"Sure, Vi," Alicia said, making another note on her yellow paper.

"I wish that you could make sure my mom would be there," Violet said quietly. "Even when she was old, she still made sure that I was taken care of. Who's going to take care of me now when I'm not here?"

"Lukas and Emily are now your legal guardians, Violet. They've talked with me a lot to prepare for your visit. They want to take care of you when you're home, just like your mom did. It will be different, because they are different people. They'll never take her place, but I know in my heart that they're willing to do everything they can for you."

"Why are they taking care of me? Why isn't Dad or Mitchell?" Violet asked Alicia, worried about her family.

"Well, your dad is getting older, too. He just turned eighty-one, and he has arthritis in his knees and hips that keeps him from getting around like he used to. Mitchell and Angie have three kids. They have their hands full, but Lukas and Emily *want* to take care of you. Everyone loves you so much, and that's just the way life has worked out," Alicia said, looking Violet in the eye.

For the first time, Violet saw Alicia in the same way she saw Kelly. She couldn't be as close to her right now as she was to Kelly, but it was only because she'd spent so much time with Kelly already. Things were changing, but that wasn't a bad thing. It just meant that life was going on.

. . .

Ian carefully pulled himself up from the leather recliner where he'd been reading for the past half hour and balanced onto his walker. He'd finally agreed to the device when he moved into Lukas and Emily's house three months ago, and only because it wasn't the traditional metal walker that he associated with old age. It had two wheels and a seat, so he could take a rest when he went out for his walks around the neighborhood, which were still important to him. He just couldn't handle the stairs anymore, and his son and daughter-in-law had a nice area downstairs that wouldn't require him to move much. His room was big, with plenty of room for his king-sized bed, recliner, television, desk, and bookcases. He looked around the room, about two hundred square feet, and realized that after eighty-one years on this earth, everything he owned was condensed to this space.

He took a deep breath as he started his long crawl to the kitchen. Glancing at the clock, he figured that Lukas and Emily would be back with Violet in the next half hour or so, and then Mitchell and Angie would arrive with their family. He smiled as he passed the kitchen appliances that Emily had perfectly lined up against the countertop and reached behind the refrigerator to unlock the custom door that his son and daughter-in-law had installed on the fridge in preparation for Violet's arrival. They'd tried so hard to make everything perfect—to ensure that she would be as comfortable here as she had been at the house she'd grown up in. The realtor told Ian that she'd had a hell of a time explaining those locked cabinets while he was showing the house. Ian chuckled at the thought of someone unfamiliar with his reality trying to make sense of the home in which he and Sam built their lives. He retrieved his water bottle from the door of the refrigerator. Emily kept it filled for him each morning, as it was easier than trying to negotiate with a new bottle's sealant or handling the heavy pitcher of filtered water that they kept in their refrigerator. Balancing the bottle on the seat of his walker, he wheeled himself into the living room, where he plopped on the couch, set his water bottle in his lap, and propped up his feet on the now-locked walker.

He heard a commotion at the front door, and while he wanted to go greet whoever was arriving, his hips argued that he should just stay in place. The front door opened, and with the commotion, he knew that Mitchell, Angie, and the kids had arrived.

"Pops?" he heard Mikey, Mitchell's youngest, call out. "Where are you, old man?"

Ian chuckled before he called back, "On the couch, young whippersnapper."

Mikey came rushing into the living room, his new sneakers squeaking on the tile floor. He was eleven, and while he was beginning to become "too cool" for all things family related, his Pops still held a special place in his heart. He sat down on the couch next to his grandfather and gave him a hug. "We get to hang out with you and Auntie Vi today." Mikey's vocal chords were starting to stretch, his voice gaining the characteristic squeak of puberty.

"Won't that be great?" Ian asked, settling his hand on his grandson's knee.

"Hey, Dad." Mitchell came in behind his son, followed by Angie and their daughters Tiffany and Tara, fifteen and thirteen, prissy and perfect—both the spitting image of their grandmother.

"Hey, Mitch." Ian waved up to his son. "Glad you could all make it today."

"Of course. Wanted to make sure that you're settling in okay. How are you?" Mitchell took the other seat next to his father.

"I'm well, Mitch. Thanks. How are you, son?" Ian smiled. His heart swelled when he thought of how much closer he and Mitchell had become since Mitchell had children of his own.

"Good. Busy as all get out. Angie's article marketing is taking off, and the kids find new ways to keep us occupied every day."

"Congratulations, Angie." Ian smiled at his daughter-in-law, and she and his granddaughters took seats on the other side of the leather sectional. "I remember those days. Enjoy them. They're gone in a flash." Ian smiled sadly, remembering when he had three teenagers in his house. It seemed so far away.

He heard the door open again, and this time, three teenagers ran to the door. "Auntie Vi!" they all said in unison. The way that they overcame their coolness to greet Ian's daughter made him smile. He was anxious to get his arms around her, too.

The entourage slowly moved into the living room, and when Violet saw her father sitting on the couch, she rushed over to him.

"Hey, Dad!" She sat down next to him and wrapped her arms around his neck.

He hugged his daughter close. He could smell the raspberry lotion that he'd sent her for her birthday, still her favorite. Samantha always made a point to ensure that Violet always had deluxe toiletries. He'd never understood why until now. To know that she smelled well taken care of comforted him, especially when he felt as though his hands were so tied regarding her care. Sam was gone, he was old, and now Lukas and Emily would be the ones who got the phone calls from Alicia about Violet. Now he was just a passive observer in his own children's lives.

"Violet, it's twelve-thirty. That means it's time for lunch. Do you want to go to the table with your nieces and nephews so that we can get started?" Emily asked. "I hung your schedule up in the dining room, and I also put a copy in your bedroom so that you'll always know what's coming next." She smiled down at her sister-in-law.

"And we're having chicken salad sandwiches with fresh fruit and pasta salad," Violet said proudly. On the car ride over, Emily had prepared her with the day's menu and assured her that it was posted along with the schedule.

"That's right. Let's get a move on." Emily ushered everyone to the dining table. She was happy to have family, as complicated as it might be. As an only child whose parents had passed away in a car accident while she was in graduate school, she needed this closeness and craziness that she'd longed for all of her life.

After a whirlwind weekend of fun, Lukas and Emily were driving Violet back to Oconomowoc on Sunday afternoon. They played Violet's favorite music, and although it was twenty years old, they all still laughed about the individual memories they found tucked between the chords of songs they'd all sung separately, at different stages of their lives.

"We had a social with all the houses, and when this song came on, everyone started dancing at the same time. Do you remember the dance that they did on the music video?" Violet was laughing. "It was so neat. Like we'd planned it, but it just happened!"

"That's so neat!" Emily agreed, laughing with her sister-in-law.

"What do you remember about this song, Em?" Violet asked her, leaning between the two front seats of the car.

"This song came out the summer I got my driver's license," Emily reminisced. "I was in band, so we had to rehearse every afternoon, and it was crazy hot. After band practice, my friends and I would go out for tacos and sing this song as loud as we could in my old car with the windows down."

"I have you both beat," Lukas said. "This song was playing my first semester as an assistant professor at UCLA. I went out for a beer with a few colleagues one night, and Dr. Brenhem, the chaired professor, had a few too many. He sang this song during karaoke. No one knew whether to clap and congratulate his gusto or just pretend that we didn't notice when it was over."

Emily doubled over with laughter at Lukas's story. "Brenhem? Really?" She had been a student at UCLA, too; that was how she'd met Lukas. "Violet, imagine a man who is about five feet tall and five feet around with a very red, very bald head. Now picture him singing *this*."

Violet cackled in the backseat. "That's great."

Lukas was pulling into the driveway of Violet's house when the laughter stopped.

"We're sure going to miss you, Vi," Emily said, getting out of the car and coming around to the backseat where her sister-in-law was opening the door.

"We are!" Lukas called out from the trunk, where he was getting Violet's bag.

"Can we start doing this once a month again?" Violet asked Emily, biting her lip in sudden fear her sister-in-law would say no.

"Of course, sweetheart. I'm so sorry that it didn't work out for a few months while we were trying to get your dad's house sold and him settled in with us. It won't happen again, I promise." Emily hugged Violet once again.

Lukas walked around to his wife and sister and wrapped his arms around them both. "My girls!" he said, squeezing them comically. Emily knew that when he took on that tone, he was trying to mask his emotions with humor.

"I'll see you in a month!" Violet called out, collecting her suitcase and walking towards the door.

"Don't you need some help with your bag? Don't you want us to walk you in?" Lukas called out to Violet's back.

"Nope. I got it. I love you!" Violet called over her shoulder, not even turning around.

"Well, that's that, I guess," Lukas looked over at Emily, a little bewildered.

"Let her go. It should make our hearts soar that she's so happy here." Emily opened the door to the car, and Lukas walked back around to the driver's seat.

Alicia was sitting in her office as Violet walked by. Violet waved through the open door, and Alicia beckoned her inside.

"What are you doing here on a Sunday?" Violet asked her.

"Just finishing up some paperwork while everyone is out doing activities." Alicia smiled and stood, hugging Violet. "How was your visit?"

"You were right," Violet said. "It was different but only because Mom wasn't there. They took care of me the same way, and I always felt safe." Violet smiled at her house manager.

"How are you feeling about coming back here after spending the weekend with your family?" Alicia asked, putting her hand on Violet's arm.

"A little sad. I have a lot of fun with my family back home. I've known them all my life. But my life actually *happens* here." Violet smiled at Alicia and picked up her suitcase. She looked out the window to see Lukas and Emily's car pulling back into the street, and she turned to go upstairs to her room.

HOW THESE BOOKS WERE CREATED

The ORP Library of disabilities books is the result of heart-felt collaboration between numerous people: the staff of ORP, including the CEO, executive director, psychologists, clinical coordinators, teachers, and more; the families of children with disabilities served by ORP, including some of the children themselves; and the Round Table Companies (RTC) storytelling team. To create these books, RTC conducted dozens of intensive, intimate interviews over a period of months and performed independent research in order to truthfully and accurately depict the lives of these families. We are grateful to all those who donated their time in support of this message, generously sharing their experience, wisdom, and—most importantly—their stories so that the books will ring true. While each story is fictional and not based on any one family or child, we could not have envisioned the world through their eyes without the access we were so lovingly given. It is our hope that in reading this uniquely personal book, you felt the spirit of everyone who contributed to its creation.

ACKNOWLEDGMENTS

The authors would like to thank the following team members at Prader-Willi Homes of Oconomowoc and ORP who generously lent their time and expertise to this book: assistant director of clinical services Rose Worden, MS, NCC, LPC, CSW; director of clinical services Susan Morris, BSW, CSW; clinical coordinator Lizabeth Moser, MSW, LCSW; director of admissions and consultative services Jackie Mallow, admissions coordinator Melanie Ignatowski, administrative assistant Jayne Gierach, and administrative assistant Rachel Gross. Your passion, experience, and wisdom make this book an invaluable tool for families, therapists, and educators. Thank you for your enthusiastic contributions to this project.

We would also like to extend our heartfelt gratitude to the parents who shared their journeys with us: Joan Black, Dr. Rob Neems, Cynthia Satko Gutkowski, Tymna Lee, David and Janet Johnson, Susan Henoch, and John Jay Coggeshall. The courage, ferocity, and love with which you shepherd your children through their lives is nothing short of heroic.

To the remarkable women who live at Prader-Willi Homes of Oconomowoc and shared their stories with us: Sophie Coggeshall, Lisa Gore, Karen Stege, Tina Soppe, Meredith, and Jenny. Thank you for letting us into your worlds, for inviting us into your times of worry, fear, desperation, determination, love, and hope. You are the reason this book exists.

And to readers of *Insatiable*—the parents committed to helping their children, the educators who teach those children skills needed for greater independence, the therapists who shine a light on what can be a frighteningly mysterious road, the schools and counties that make difficult financial decisions to benefit these children, and finally, those who live with Prader-Willi Syndrome each day: thank you. You inspire us.

DEBBIE FRISK, BS, BSW, MSW

BIOGRAPHY

For forty years, Debbie Frisk has worked with children, adults, and families in a variety of settings in the human services field, including acute medical and psychiatric hospitals, long-term care facilities, veteran's hospitals and rehabilitation centers, community-based group home programs, in-home services programs, public schools, juvenile corrections, and intensive residential treatment facilities.

Although she has worked with a wide variety of populations, Debbie's absolute niche is working with children and young adults with developmental and emotional disabilities, severe behavioral disabilities, autism spectrum disorders, dual diagnoses, and complex, co-occurring multiple disabilities. Her particular expertise is in a variety of low incidence syndromes and neurological and genetic disorders, including Prader-Willi Syndrome.

As a consultant for *Insatiable*, Debbie tapped into her education and vast experience to help bring to life the pain and challenges faced by children with Prader-Willi Syndome and their families. She has a dual degree in psychology and social welfare from Carroll College (now University), and a master's degree in social work with a specialization in clinical–physical and mental health from University of Wisconsin-Milwaukee.

After working in all aspects of residential treatment at ORP, Debbie now serves as a vice president for the organization. Utilizing her clinical background and keen understanding of governmental social services systems and special education systems and laws, she helps her clients navigate bureaucratic hurdles to find and receive the most optimal treatment options possible and to secure funding for those services.

Debbie has had the privilege of working with numerous teams of people throughout the years, all of whom have shared the vision, mission, constancy of purpose, and commitment to providing compassionate quality services with a goal of assisting people to achieve their maximum potential and to live as independently as possible.

CHELSEA McCUTCHIN

BIOGRAPHY

Chelsea McCutchin is a wordsmith who believes strongly in everyone's power to listen, act, and change the world. She graduated from The University of Texas at Austin with a degree in English and creative writing, before convincing her native Texan husband and son to come back home to Florida with her. This is Chelsea's second book with ORP, and she is beyond blessed to be the catalyst bringing the remarkable and interesting world of Prader-Willi Syndrome into the greater vernacular.

KATIE GUTIERREZ

BIOGRAPHY

Katie Gutierrez believes that a well-told story can transcend what a reader "knows" to be real about the world—and thus change the world for that reader. In every form, story is transformative, and Katie is proud to spend her days immersed in it as executive editor for Round Table Companies, Inc.

Since 2007, Katie has edited approximately 50 books and co-written several of the ORP Library of disabilities books, including *Meltdown* and *An Unlikely Trust*. She has been humbled by the stories she has heard and hopes these books will help guide families on their often-lonely journeys, connecting them with resources and support. She also hopes they will give the general population a glimpse into the Herculean jobs taken on so fiercely by parents, doctors, therapists, educators, and others who live with, work with, and love children like Violet.

Katie holds a BA in English and philosophy from Southwestern University and an MFA in fiction from Texas State University. She has contributed to or been profiled in publications including *Forbes*, *Entrepreneur* magazine, *People* magazine, *Hispanic Executive Quarterly*, and *Narrative* magazine. She can't believe she's lucky enough to do what she loves every day.

JAMES G. BALESTRIERI

BIOGRAPHY

James G. Balestrieri is currently the CEO of Oconomowoc Residential Programs, Inc. (ORP). He has worked in the human services field for 40 years, holding positions that run the gamut to include assistant maintenance, assistant cook, direct care worker, teacher's aide, summer camp counselor, bookkeeper, business administrator, marketing director, CFO, and CEO. Jim graduated from Marquette University with a B.S. in Business Administration (1977) and a Master's in Business Administration with an emphasis in Marketing (1988). He is also a Certified Public Accountant (Wisconsin—1982). Jim has a passion for creatively addressing the needs of those with impairments by managing the inherent stress among funding, programming, and profitability. He believes that those with a disability enjoy rights and protections that were created by the hard-fought efforts of those who came before them; that the Civil Rights movement is not just for minority groups; and that people with disabilities have a right to find their place in the world and to achieve their maximum potential as individuals. For more information, see *www.orp.com.*

ABOUT ORP

Oconomowoc Residential Programs, Inc. is an employee-owned family of companies whose mission is to make a difference in the lives of people with disabilities. Our dedicated staff of 2,000 employee owners provides quality services and professional care to more than 1,700 children, adolescents, and adults with special needs. ORP provides a continuum of care, including residential therapeutic education, community-based residential services, support services, respite care, treatment programs, and day services. The individuals in our care include people with developmental disabilities, physical disabilities, and intellectual disabilities. **Our guiding principle is passion:** a passion for the people we serve and for the work we do. For a comprehensive look at our programs and people, please visit *www.orp.com*.

ORP offers residential therapeutic education programs and alternative day schools among its array of services. These programs offer developmentally appropriate education and treatment for children, adolescents, and young adults in settings specially attuned to their needs. We provide special programs for students with specific academic and social issues relative to a wide range of disabilities, including autistic disorder, Asperger's disorder, mental retardation, anxiety disorders, depression, bipolar disorder, reactive attachment disorder, attention deficit disorder, Prader-Willi Syndrome, and other disabilities.

Genesee Lake School is a nationally recognized provider of comprehensive residential treatment, educational, and vocational services for children, adolescents, and young adults with emotional, mental health, neurological, or developmental disabilities. GLS has specific expertise in Autism Spectrum Disorders, anxiety and mood disorders, and behavioral disorders. We provide an individualized, person-centered, integrated team approach, which emphasizes positive behavioral support, therapeutic relationships, and developmentally appropriate practices. Our goal is to assist each individual to acquire skills to live, learn, and succeed in a community-based, less restrictive environment. GLS is particularly known for its high quality educational services for residential and day school students.

Genesee Lake School / Admissions Director
36100 Genesee Lake Road
Oconomowoc, WI 53066
262-569-5510
http://www.geneseelakeschool.com

T.C. Harris Academy is a private school option, in the local community, that works not only to stabilize a student's behavior in a therapeutic setting, but also help them thrive academically. Our goal is simple: provide students with the skills they need to function effectively and achieve greater success.

T.C. Harris Academy
3746 Rome Drive
Lafayette, IN 47905
765-448-9989
http://www.tcharris.com

T.C. Harris School is located in an attractive setting in Lafayette, Indiana. T.C. Harris teaches skills to last a lifetime, through a full therapeutic program as well as day school and other services.

T.C. Harris School / Admissions Director
3700 Rome Drive
Lafayette, IN 47905
765-448-4220
http://www.tcharris.com

Transitions Academy provides behavioral health and educational services to adolescents in a 24-hour structured residential setting. Treatment services are offered that are best practice and evidence based, targeting social, emotional, behavioral, and mental health impairments. Transitions Academy serves children from throughout the United States.

Transitions Academy / Admissions Director
11075 North Pennsylvania Street
Indianapolis, IN 46280
Toll Free: 1-844-488-0448
admissions@transitions-academy.com

The Richardson School is a day school in West Allis, Wisconsin that provides an effective, positive alternative education environment serving children from Milwaukee, Beloit, and their surrounding communities.

The Richardson School / Director
6753 West Roger Street
West Allis, WI 53219
414-540-8500
http://www.richardsonschool.com

RESOURCES

For further learning and support, the authors of this book recommend the following resources.

BOOKS, FILMS, AND CURRICULA

Butler, Merlin G., Phillip D. K. Lee, and Barbara Y. Whitman. *Management of Prader-Willi Syndrome, Third Edition.* New York: Springer Science + Business Media, Inc., 2006. With chapters contributed by 32 experts in the care of individuals with PWS.

Champagne, Marilyn P., RN MSW, and Walker-Hrisch, Leslie, IMEd., FAAIDD. *Circles: Intimacy & Relationships, Level 1.* Available through James Stanfield. Curriculum includes six DVDs, 107 minutes of instruction, one giant wall graph, 50 large laminated graph icons, 50 student personal graphs, 300 peel-and-stick icons, and a teacher's guide.

Davis, Nancy, Ph.D. *Once Upon a Time: Therapeutic Stories that Teach and Heal.* Burke, VA: Nancy Davis, Ph.D. 2006.

Food, Behavior and Beyond; Practical Management for the Child and Adult with PWS. DVD. Pittsburgh: Prader-Willi Syndrome Association USA, 2008. Featuring expert speakers Janice Forster, M.D. and Linda Gourash, M.D.

Forster, M.D., Janice. *Best Practice Guidelines for Standard of Care in PWS.* Hubert Soyer, Ph.D., and Norbert Hodebeck Stunteback, 2010. Created by the IPWSO Caregiver Conferences 2008 and 2009. Presentations, abstracts, and guidelines for presenting standards of care in over 80 nations.

Heinemann, Janalee. *Prader-Willi Syndrome Is What I Have Not Who I Am!*. Sarasota: PWSA (USA) publication, Coastal Printing, Inc., 2004.

WEBSITES AND ORGANIZATIONS

Americans With Disabilities Act (ADA), *http://ada.gov.*

"IDEA – Building the Legacy: IDEA 2004," *http://idea.ed.gov.*

International Prader-Willi Syndrome Organisation (IPWSO), *http://www.ipwso.org.*

Prader-Willi Syndrome Association USA (PWSAUSA), *http://pwsausa.org.* To find a local chapter, visit *http://www.pwsausa.org/find-local-chapter.*

Prader-Willi Syndrome Association of Wisconsin, *http://pwsaofwi.org.*

National Organization of Rare Diseases (NORD), *http://rarediseases.org.*

Office of Rare Diseases Research (ORDR), *http://rarediseases.info.nih.gov.*

The Children's Institute of Pittsburgh, *http://www.amazingkids.org.*

OTHER RESOURCES

State-specific departments of:
Human or Social Services
Developmental/Intellectual Disabilities
Mental Health
Child Welfare/Children's Services
Family Services

State-specific local education agencies, school districts, and special education cooperatives:
State Boards of Education

PRADER-WILLI SYNDROME

Estimated to occur once in every 15,000 births, Prader-Willi Syndrome is a rare genetic disorder that includes features of cognitive disabilities, problem behaviors, and, most pervasively, chronic hunger that leads to dangerous overeating and its life-threatening consequences. *Insatiable: A Prader-Willi Story* and its companion comic book, *Ultra-Violet: One Girl's Prader-Willi Story*, draw on dozens of intensive interviews to offer insight into the world of those struggling with Prader-Willi Syndrome. Both books tell the fictional story of Violet, a vivacious young girl born with the disorder, and her family, who—with the help of experts—will not give up their quest to give her a healthy and happy life.

INSATIABLE
A PRADER-WILLI STORY

ULTRA-VIOLET
ONE GIRL'S PRADER-WILLI STORY

ASPERGER'S DISORDER

Meltdown and its companion comic book, *Melting Down*, are both based on the fictional story of Benjamin, a boy diagnosed with Asperger's disorder and additional challenging behavior. From the time Benjamin is a toddler, he and his parents know he is different: he doesn't play with his sister, refuses to make eye contact, and doesn't communicate well with others. And his tantrums are not like normal tantrums; they're meltdowns that will eventually make regular schooling—and day-to-day life—impossible. Both the prose book, intended for parents, educators, and mental health professionals, and the comic for the kids themselves demonstrate that the journey toward hope isn't simple . . . but with the right tools and teammates, it's possible.

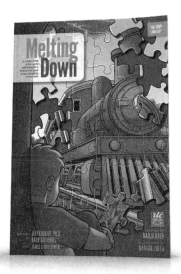

MELTDOWN

ASPERGER'S DISORDER,
CHALLENGING BEHAVIOR,
AND A FAMILY'S JOURNEY
TOWARD HOPE

MELTING DOWN

A COMIC FOR KIDS WITH
ASPERGER'S DISORDER AND
CHALLENGING BEHAVIOR

AUTISM SPECTRUM DISORDER

Mr. Incredible shares the fictional story of Adam, a boy diagnosed with autistic disorder. On Adam's first birthday, his mother recognizes that something is different about him: he recoils from the touch of his family, preferring to accept physical contact only in the cool water of the family's pool. As Adam grows older, he avoids eye contact, is largely nonverbal, and has very specific ways of getting through the day; when those habits are disrupted, intense meltdowns and self-harmful behavior follow. From seeking a diagnosis to advocating for special education services, from keeping Adam safe to discovering his strengths, his family becomes his biggest champion. The journey to realizing Adam's potential isn't easy, but with hope, love, and the right tools and teammates, they find that Adam truly is *Mr. Incredible*. The companion comic in this series, inspired by social stories, offers an innovative, dynamic way to guide children—and parents, educators, and caregivers—through some of the daily struggles experienced by those with autism.

MR. INCREDIBLE

A STORY ABOUT AUTISM,
OVERCOMING CHALLENGING
BEHAVIOR, AND A FAMILY'S FIGHT
FOR SPECIAL EDUCATION RIGHTS

INCREDIBLE ADAM
AND A DAY WITH AUTISM

AN ILLUSTRATED STORY
INSPIRED BY SOCIAL NARRATIVES

BULLYING

Nearly one third of all school children face physical, verbal, social, or cyber bullying on a regular basis. Educators and parents search for ways to end bullying, but as that behavior becomes more sophisticated, it's harder to recognize and stop. In *Classroom Heroes*, Jason is a quiet, socially awkward seventh grader who has long suffered bullying in silence. His parents notice him becoming angrier and more withdrawn, but they don't realize the scope of the problem until one bully takes it too far—and one teacher acts on her determination to stop it. Both *Classroom Heroes* and *How to Be a Hero*—along with a supporting coloring book (*Heroes in the Classroom*) and curriculum guide (*Those Who Bully and Those Who Are Bullied*)—recognize that stopping bullying requires a change in mindset: adults and children must create a community that simply does not tolerate bullying. These books provide practical yet very effective strategies to end bullying, one student at a time.

CLASSROOM HEROES

ONE CHILD'S STRUGGLE
WITH BULLYING AND
A TEACHER'S MISSION TO
CHANGE SCHOOL CULTURE

HOW TO BE A HERO

A COMIC BOOK
ABOUT BULLYING

FAMILY SUPPORT

Schuyler Walker was just four years old when he was diagnosed with autism, bipolar disorder, and ADHD. In 2004, childhood mental illness was rarely talked about or understood. With knowledge and resources scarce, Schuyler's mom, Christine, navigated a lonely maze to determine what treatments, medications, and therapies could benefit her son. In the ten years since his diagnosis, Christine has often wished she had a "how to" guide that would provide the real mom-to-mom information she needed to survive the day and, in the end, help her family navigate the maze with knowledge, humor, grace, and love. Christine may not have had a manual at the beginning of her journey, but she hopes this book will serve as yours.

CHASING HOPE
YOUR COMPASS FOR A NEW NORMAL
NAVIGATING THE WORLD
OF THE SPECIAL NEEDS CHILD

REACTIVE ATTACHMENT DISORDER

An Unlikely Trust: Alina's Story of Adoption, Complex Trauma, Healing, and Hope, and its companion children's book, *Alina's Story*, share the journey of Alina, a young girl adopted from Russia. After living in an orphanage during her early life, Alina is unequipped to cope with the complexities of the outside world. She has a deep mistrust of others and finds it difficult to talk about her feelings. When she is frightened, overwhelmed, or confused, she lashes out in rages that scare her family. Alina's parents know she needs help and work endlessly to find it for her, eventually discovering a special school that will teach Alina new skills. Slowly, Alina gets better at expressing her feelings and solving problems. For the first time in her life, she realizes she is truly safe and loved . . . and capable of loving in return.

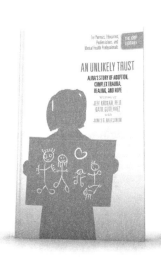 

AN UNLIKELY TRUST
ALINA'S STORY OF ADOPTION, COMPLEX TRAUMA, HEALING, AND HOPE

ALINA'S STORY
LEARNING HOW TO TRUST, HEAL, AND HOPE

Also look for books on children and psychotropic medications coming soon!